Complete guide to looking after your baby

igloobooks

Published in 2015
by Igloo Books Ltd
Cottage Farm
Sywell
NN6 0BJ
www.igloobooks.com

GUA006 0215
2 4 6 8 10 9 7 5 3 1
ISBN 978-1-78440-151-1

Printed and manufactured in China

Note: This book is intended as a helpful and informative guide on looking after your baby and is
sold with the understanding that the author and publisher are not engaged in rendering any
personal professional services. This book is not designed to be a comprehensive medical book
and the reader should always consult a doctor or midwife in all matters relating to health. The author and
publisher disclaim all responsibility for any liability, loss or risk, personal or otherwise, that is incurred
as a consequence, directly or indirectly, of the use and application of any of the contents of this book.

Contents

Foreword

Becoming a parent is without any doubt one of the most rewarding things that can happen to people, but it is also confusing, scary, daunting, frustrating and exhausting for both the parents and the baby. There are plenty of people willing to give advice, not all of it useful! There are possibly as many opinions on parenting and bringing up babies as there are parents in the world.

As a midwife I have seen thousands of parents mystified about how to deal with this new person they have been let loose with. Most new parents can`t believe they have been "allowed" home with such a precious object without some sort of state supervision. As a new parent I felt exactly the same emotions and I had hundreds of hours of experience with newborn babies. After twenty years as a midwife and working with new parents I have come to only two firm conclusions. There is no such thing as a "bad" baby. I also firmly believe it`s impossible to "spoil" a baby. There are only frustrated and befuddled parents who are not confident they have the skills or experience in order to be successful in their new role.

Most of us, as parents, want some good sensible advice that is somewhere in the middle ground of what is accepted to be good enough parenting. We want to make sure our children are safe, secure and loved and able to thrive in our care.

This book will help provide that as it has lots of good sensible advice based on the most up to date evidence available. It is a comprehensive guide for the journey into parenthood. The information contained within it will give you confidence and answers when you need it most. It dosen't have every answer for every eventuality (no book or parent has that despite what your mother-in-law might say) but it does provide a well written and illustrated guide to the basics of baby and infant care.

Knowledge is indeed power and armed with the knowledge within these pages you will feel more confident and assured in your parenting skills. This will reduce the stress often associated with becoming a new parent. Therefore you will enjoy your journey into parenthood more and have the ability to savour every moment.

Parenting is a thrilling rollercoaster of a mixture of emotions which challenge your skills, abilities and experience every day. I wish you the very best of luck with your baby and I hope this book becomes an invaluable friend and source of support when you need it most.

Lee Wright RN RM BSc, MSc

Before
the
Birth

Shopping for your baby

Shopping for your baby can be one of the most exciting parts of expecting a baby – as well as the most stressful! Before you start to buy, make a realistic list of all the things you want. Try talking to friends who have children to see what they recommend. It's likely they'll all have things they bought and realised they didn't need, as well as things that they couldn't live without.

Take it slowly – you don't need to buy everything straight away. Babies need clothes and nappies, somewhere to sleep, some form of transport, and milk. If you can do this, you've got it covered!

Clothes

You'll be changing your baby's clothing several times a day, so make sure outfits are simple and open easily for nappy changes. It's hard to predict which size clothing your baby will need. Many outgrow 'newborn' or '0 to 3 month' clothes very quickly and some babies skip out the 'newborn' size altogether. Some babies, even if they are born on their due date, may need 'premature' baby clothes. The best tip is to buy clothing in several sizes, keep the receipt, and return what you don't use.

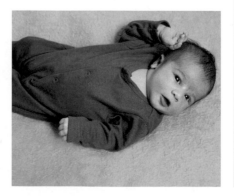

You will need:

- Six sleepsuits (all-in-ones with long sleeves and legs with feet).

- Six vests (bodysuits with short sleeves and no legs) – these can be worn alone or under a sleepsuit, depending on the temperature.

- Two cardigans.

- Newborn hat, bootees or socks.

- Scratch mittens – some babies have a habit of scratching their faces.

You may want to buy:

- A warm all-in-one snowsuit (winter babies only!)

- Sunhat with a wide brim (summer babies only!)

Travel

There are a lot of different styles of pushchairs and prams available and the choice can seem overwhelming. The best idea is to go to a large store and try some out to see what you like. Staff will advise you, and can help you choose something to suit your lifestyle and price range. For example, will you be travelling a lot by car, or will you want something that goes easily on a bus? Do you need something that folds up small to save space?

Remember, your newborn baby will not be able to sit up in a pushchair for several months. Babies need to lie flat until they can sit up unaided. It is recommended that a newborn baby does not sit in an infant car seat for longer than two hours at a time.

Feeding

If you are breastfeeding and plan to express you will need:

✸ Bottles and teats

✸ Steriliser

✸ Bottle brush

✸ Breast pump

You may also want to buy:

✸ Bottle warmer

✸ Muslin cloths

If you decide to bottle feed you will need:

✸ Formula milk

✸ Bottles and teats

✸ Steriliser

✸ Bottle brush

You could choose:

An all-in-one travel system – this comes as a set with a wheeled base and interchangeable seats:

OR

An infant car seat + a pushchair that can be used from birth (has the option to lie flat)

1. A carrycot (so your newborn can lie flat).

2. A pushchair seat (to use when your baby can sit up unaided).

OR

An infant car seat + a pram. (If your pram doesn't convert into a pushchair, you will need to buy one when your baby can sit up)

3. An infant car seat, which can be used in the car, then carried from the car and attached to the base (instead of the carrycot or pushchair seat) to make a buggy.

You may want to buy:

✸ Baby carrier such as a sling or wrap for holding your baby close to you.

✸ Pram sheet – to help keep it clean.

✸ Pram blanket – to wrap up your baby when out and about.

✸ Rain cover if not included with buggy.

✸ Sunshade for summer.

Note: You will need to bring an infant car seat to the hospital if you are heading home in a car or taxi.

Baby names

Choosing a name for your baby can be fun – or the cause of many arguments. Baby name likes and dislikes are personal things, and many people refuse to let anyone know in advance what name they are planning on, in case it is laughed at – or stolen. If you and your partner really can't agree, buy a book of baby names and draw up a shortlist of the ones you both don't mind. There may be names that you both like that you just haven't thought of yet.

Say the name out loud to see if you like it – and work out what it is likely to be shortened to. If you can't bear the shortened version, don't pick the name. You won't be able to stop school friends or relatives using it.

If you are choosing a name from another language, make sure that you know what it means. Even if the word sounds beautiful, it could mean something you don't want it to!

An unusual spelling might seem like a good idea, but in reality you are condemning your baby to a life of explaining over the phone that her name is spelled Sharlotteh and pronounced Charlotte.

A name that sounds cute as a baby may not sound so cute for an adult. Try imagining your grown-up child introducing herself to a potential boss at a job interview.

Make sure that the name works with your surname. Peter is a great name, and Piper is a common surname. But Peter Piper may get teased. It's also not great to pick two words that rhyme or sound too similar, such as Jane Lane or Phoebe Beamer.

Try to avoid names that have already been used by friends or family members for their babies – even if they say they don't mind, they are probably just being polite.

Don't forget that if you pick a middle name for your baby, her initials may spell something you don't want – such as Bella Una Matthews.

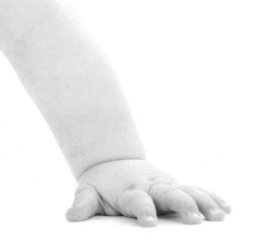

Popular baby names from around the world:

Boys

Africa – Afiya, Ade, Kazi, Kofi, Zaire
Australia – Lachlan, Cooper, Riley, Noah, Thomas
Brazil – Gabriel, Davi, Miguel, Lucas, Pedro
France – Lucus, Enzo, Yanis, Hugo, Mathis
Germany – Lukas, Jonas, Felix, Louis, Leon
India – Aryan, Sai, Ishaan, Krishna, Aarav
Russia – Alexandr, Maxim, Ivan, Artem, Nikita
Spain – Santiago, Sebastian, Samuel, Diego, Ben
UK – Oliver, Jack, Harry, Charlie, James
USA - Aiden, Jackson, Ethan, Jayden, Liam

Girls

Africa – Halle, Kya, Asha, Imani, Aliyah
Australia – Sienna, Ruby, Jessica, Grace, Zoe
Brazil – Julia, Beatriz, Manuela, Rafaela, Gabriela
Canada – Ava, Madison, Charlotte, Aubrey, Ella
France – Lola, Lea, Clara, Ines, Jade
Germany – Mia, Lena, Leonie, Hannah, Sarah
India – Ananya, Jiya, Anika, Anushka, Khushi
Russia – Anastasia, Helina, Eva, Ekaterina, Daria
Spain – Camila, Valeria, Daniella, Maria, Valentina
UK – Lily, Emily, Isabella, Sophia, Olivia
USA – Addison, Chloe, Emma, Abigail, Harper

Illegal names

In New Zealand, there is a law banning names which could cause offence. Nine-year-old Talula Does The Hula From Hawaii was renamed by a judge during a custody battle. In 1991, a Swedish couple tried to call their son Brfxxccxxmnpccccllllmmnprxvclmnckssqlbb11116 (pronounced Albin) as a protest against Sweden's strict naming laws.

Bathing

You will need:

- Washcloths
- Hooded bath towel
- Soft sponges

You may want to buy:

- Non-slip bath mat
- Baby bath – although your baby can use the big bath, share with you, or you could even use a new washing-up bowl at the very beginning.
- Baby wash – many people choose to clean with water and cotton wool for the first few weeks
- Baby nail clippers
- Baby brush and comb

Sleeping

Make sure you have enough bedding as it can get dirty quite quickly! Pillows are not safe to use until your baby is over 12 months old.

You will need:

- Cot (with mattress)
- Sheets and blankets
- Baby monitor – if your baby will be sleeping in a room away from you

You may also want to buy:

- Moses basket – these are lovely for small babies, but your baby will grow out of it.
- Crib – this is smaller than a cot, and will fit well beside your bed, but may be an unnecessary expense.
- A 'white noise' machine – some people find these invaluable in soothing restless babies.
- Musical cot mobile.

Playtime

Your newborn baby won't need toys for a while, and the chances are you will be getting a lot of these as presents from friends and relatives.

You may want to buy:

- Bouncer chair – it's good to have somewhere safe to put your baby down
- Play mat or play gym

Useful extras

- A dummy – you don't have to use it, but you might be pleased you have it!
- Non biological washing powder
- Smoke alarm for baby's room
- Digital thermometer – for checking if your baby has a fever

New mother care

- Big box of extra-long maxi pads
- Breast pads
- Nursing nightgown or pyjamas
- Nursing bras (1-2 comfy nursing bras plus one to sleep in)

Changing time

You will need:

- Newborn nappies in several sizes.
- Nappy sacks – for disposal of nappies.
- Changing mat.
- Baby wipes.
- Cotton wool.
- Barrier cream – to prevent nappy rash.

You may want to buy:

- Changing table.
- Changing bag – to keep all your baby's things together when you go out.
- Mini changing mat – to keep in your bag for trips out. Most baby changing bags come with these included.

11

Your ★ Newborn

Your baby's development

Your baby is growing and changing all the time. During her first year, she will learn more than at any other time in her life. It is enjoyable and useful to watch out for early childhood milestones, but be careful about being competitive, or worrying that your baby is getting left behind – babies meet milestones at their own pace. If your baby was premature, she will need a bit more time. You can talk to your health visitor if you have any concerns.

Week one

It is usual for your baby to be very sleepy for the first few days of her life. Take advantage of this time to get some rest yourself. Your baby will keep her fists clenched shut and her arms and legs curled in just as she did in the womb, and it will take a few weeks for this position to relax.

Week two

Your baby's eyes can only focus about 8 to 10 inches from her face. This is approximately the distance she is from her mother's face while she's breastfeeding. Her hearing is developing and she may turn her head to the direction your voice is coming from.

Week three

Your baby's arms and legs are getting less jerky, she may start to make more eye contact with you, and even try to lift her head when lying on her tummy. The stump of her umbilical cord may have fallen off by now, so you can give her a first bath!

Week four

By week four, your baby may gurgle, hum, grunt or coo. Try talking back to her to keep her amused – babies love hearing the sound of your voice. She may be discovering her fingers and toes and playing with them or sucking them for comfort.

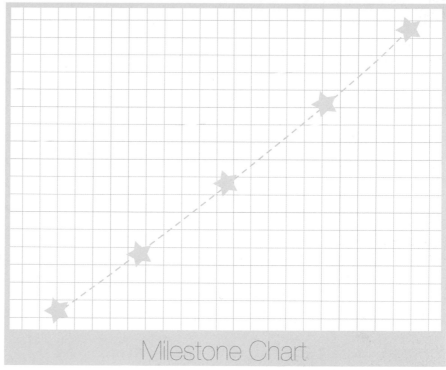

Your baby will start to make a wider range of sounds.

Your baby will try to lift her head, when lying on her tummy.

Your baby will get back to, or surpass, her birth weight.

Your baby will have a spontaneous smile (not a social smile).

Your baby may be startled by loud noises.

Milestone Chart

| Newborn | 1 week | 2 weeks | 3 weeks | 4 weeks |

Your baby's reflexes

Your baby is born with several automatic responses that help her to cope with life outside the womb. Some of these will slowly disappear over the first few months of her life.

Sucking reflex – this is crucial for your baby's survival and means that she will automatically suck on your nipple, the teat of a bottle or your finger.

Rooting reflex – this helps your baby find food. If you tickle the side of her cheek, she will turn towards you and try to suck your finger.

Grasping reflex – just place your finger in your baby's hand and she will grasp it tightly. If you try to move your finger, she will grasp even tighter.

Startle (Moro) reflex – if your baby hears a loud noise,

Walking (stepping) reflex – hold your baby upright under her arms and let her feet touch the floor. She will make natural stepping movements.

Diving reflex – if you place your baby underwater, she'll swim happily because her lungs automatically seal off. Do not attempt to try this out unless you are with a qualified baby swimming instructor.

Note: Never leave your baby unattended to swim underwater.

Holding your new baby

It's understandable that you may feel nervous about picking up your baby for the first time. Newborn babies seem very fragile and vulnerable, but don't be afraid to hold them firmly. Babies like to feel secure and enjoy being close to the warmth of your body. It won't take long before holding your baby feels like the most natural thing in the world – and your baby will love being held close to you.

Follow these basic rules:

✴ Wash your hands – newborn babies have not yet had a chance to develop strong immune systems.

✴ Support the head and neck at all times – cradle the head when you carry your baby and support it when you lay him down.

✴ Keep your movements smooth and gentle – your baby may be scared at being moved suddenly from one position to another.

✴ Hold your baby securely – if you feel confident, she will too. If you hold her away from your body, she may not feel very secure.

✴ Never shake a newborn baby – her neck muscles are not strong enough to hold her head up unaided. Shaking can cause bleeding in the brain or even death.

✴ Remember that a newborn baby is not ready for rough play yet. Do not jog her on your knee or swing her in the air.

How to pick up a baby who is lying on his back:

Use both hands to scoop her up, using one hand to support her bottom and holding the other against her head.
OR
Lift her up under the arms, resting your fingers on the back of her head.
THEN
Turn her so that she lies cradled in your arms, with her head in the crook of your elbow.

Four simple ways to hold your baby:

Cradle hold

This is the simplest hold for a newborn baby. Place your baby's head in the crook of your arm, then wrap the other arm around her. She should feel comforted and secure. This is the position that an older sibling or cousin should use if they want to have a turn at holding the new baby. Never force children to hold a baby if they don't want to, or allow a young child to hold a baby unattended.

Shoulder hold

Lean your baby against your shoulder and wrap your arm (the one on the side she is leaning on) around her bottom. Use the other arm to hold her back or support her neck. Babies often sleep well in this position. They can hear your hearbeat and your breathing which is comforting.

Face down

Position your baby's head over the crook of your elbow, using your forearm to support her body. Put your other hand between her legs to support her tummy. This is a great position for helping a baby get rid of gas as the pressure on his tummy can help him to burp! You can gently rock her in this position to soothe her.

Lap hold

Sitting with your knees together, lay your baby on her back. Her head should be resting on your knees and her feet against your tummy. This is a useful position to use when your arms get tired. It also means you can spend time looking at your baby's face and interacting with her.

Feeding your baby

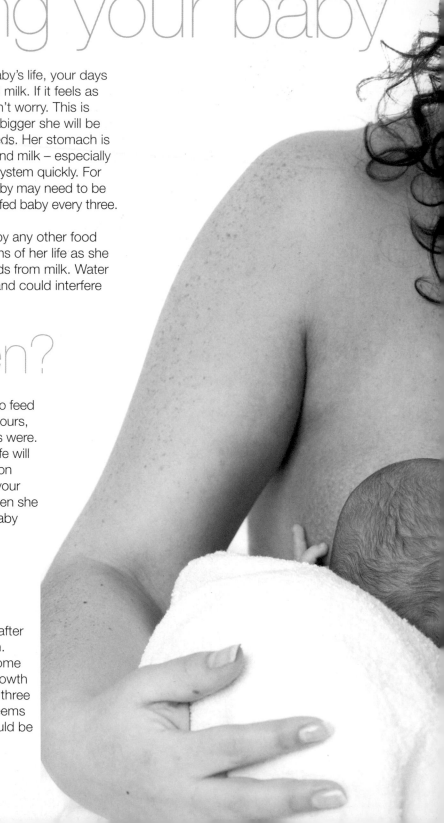

For the first few weeks of your baby's life, your days – and nights – will revolve around milk. If it feels as if you are feeding all the time, don't worry. This is normal, and as your baby grows bigger she will be able to go for longer between feeds. Her stomach is only about the size of a walnut, and milk – especially breastmilk – passes through her system quickly. For the first few weeks a breastfed baby may need to be fed every two hours, and a bottle fed baby every three.

There is no need to give your baby any other food or drink during the first few months of her life as she gets all the nourishment she needs from milk. Water will overfill your baby's stomach and could interfere with her weight gain.

How often?

Mothers used to be encouraged to feed on a rigid schedule of every four hours, no matter how hungry their babies were. Today, your health visitor or midwife will advise you to feed your newborn on demand. This means listening to your baby's signals and feeding her when she is hungry. Some signs that your baby could be hungry are:

- Fussing
- Sucking on her fist
- Rooting around for a nipple

If your baby seems hungry soon after a feed, you should feed her again. Babies can just be hungrier on some days than others. Babies have growth spurts at around five weeks, and three months. If your baby suddenly seems to be feeding more often, this could be the reason.

Is my baby thriving?

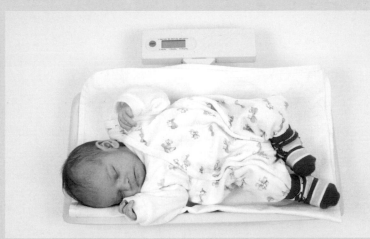

Make sure that your baby regularly sees your health visitor who can plot her growth on a chart, which compares her weight with a national average. For example, if your baby is in the 60th percentile for weight, it means that 40% of babies the same age as yours will weigh more and 60% will weigh less. Don't worry if your baby is in a low or high percentile. It is more important that your baby grows steadily along her own curve. If your baby is thriving she will be:

* Steadily gaining weight.
* Having frequent dirty nappies.
* Have a good skin colour and bright eyes.
* Seem satisfied after feeding.

Note: If you are at all worried about the length of time between feeds, chat to your midwife or health visitor. They will advise you on what is best for your baby.

Some very young babies are too sleepy to wake up and demand food, for example if they were born prematurely, have been affected by drugs used during labour, or are jaundiced or sick. If this is the case, you should wake her every three hours to feed, and keep a careful eye on her weight gain.

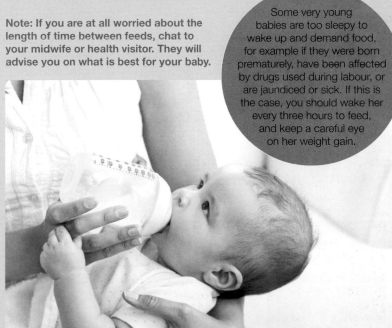

Breastfeeding essentials

Breast milk is the perfect food for your baby and contains everything he needs for the first months of his life. It can protect him from infections and diseases, and also has health benefits for the new mother.

Your baby's first feed

Colostrum is a concentrated yellow-coloured milk produced during late pregnancy. It is packed with antibodies that boost your baby's immune system and contains all the protein, minerals, fats and vitamins he needs. If you decide to bottle feed, your midwife will still encourage breastfeeding for the first few days, so that your baby can have this special nourishment.

After two or three days, the colostrum stops and the breast milk 'comes in.' The mother's breasts may become engorged and feel hot, heavy and painful to touch and she may get a temperature. It won't last more than a few days and can be relieved with a mild painkiller such as paracetamol or ibuprofen. Breast pads worn inside the bra can stop milk leaking out and should be changed at every feed.

How does it work?

As the baby sucks, the nerve endings of the nipple and areola are stimulated and send signals to the mother's brain which releases the hormones oxytocin and prolactin. Oxytocin starts the milk flowing into the baby's mouth and prolactin makes sure that more milk is produced and stored. This is because milk supply works on a supply-and-demand basis. The more you feed, the more milk you make.

Peel off a large green cabbage leaf and place it in your bra, against your skin, to help soothe the uncomfortable feeling of breast engorgement.

Foremilk and hindmilk

Mature breast milk is made up of two types of milk. Foremilk is produced when you start feeding your baby. It is thin and watery and quenches your baby's thirst. As your baby carries on sucking, hindmilk is produced. This is the rich milk that gives your baby energy and helps him to grow. It is important to make sure that your baby empties the whole breast or he will quickly become hungry again.

Breastfeeding steps

Breastfeeding is a skill that has to be learnt, and although some women pick it up easily, some find it harder than others. There is a lot of support available for women who want to breastfeed but are having problems. Your health visitor or midwife will be able to help, or recommend a breastfeeding counsellor or a breastfeeding support group. Joining a group is a great way to meet other mothers in a similar situation.

Some parents worry that breastfeeding will make it harder for their partner to bond with their baby. However there are plenty of ways to bond, such as bathing, changing nappies and carrying the baby in a sling. A supportive partner can help prepare meals for a breastfeeding mother, bring her water to drink while she feeds and later, feed the baby with expressed milk.

How to boost your milk supply:

Eat a balanced diet that includes protein and calcium

You need an extra 500 calories a day while breastfeeding

Keep up your fluid levels by drinking water

Avoid caffeine and alcohol as these will pass to your baby through your milk

If you feel uncomfortable about breastfeeding in public, drape a light scarf or a muslin over your shoulder so it covers your breast and baby.

Positions for breastfeeding

1. This is the classic cradle position where your baby is held against the front of your body, cradled in your arms.

2. The underarm or football position is useful if you have large breasts, or are recovering from a caesarean. You can tuck a pillow under your arm to support your baby.

3. Use the side-lying position if you are very tired, or are recovering from a caesarean or find it uncomfortable to sit.

Step by Step

1. Sit comfortably, making sure that your back is supported. You may want to put your baby on a pillow, or rest your feet on a cushion so your lap is flat.

2. Place your nipple between your baby's upper lip and nose and encourage her to open her mouth by gently brushing her upper lip with your nipple.

3. When your baby starts rooting, pull her to your breast. (Don't bring your breast to her mouth.)

4. As your baby latches on, she should get a big mouthful of breast – a baby sucking just on a nipple can be painful! If it hurts, gently detach your baby by putting your little finger in the corner of her mouth to break the suction, and start again.

If your baby is correctly positioned:

- She will have a mouthful of breast including the nipple and much of the areola.

- There should be more of the underside of the areola in her mouth than the top.

- Her jaw muscles will work rhythmically, as far back as her ears.

- Her cheeks will be plump – if they are hollowed as she sucks, she is not properly latched on.

5. Hold your baby close and support her neck as she feeds.

6. Your baby will let you know that the breast is empty by falling asleep, letting the nipple slide out of her mouth or starting to play with it. You can then offer the other breast.

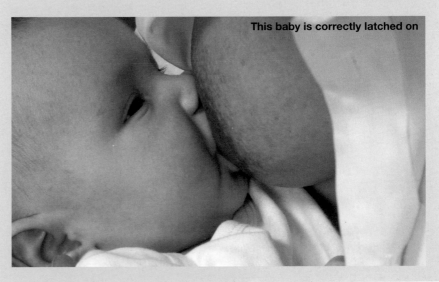

This baby is correctly latched on

Bottle feeding

Feeding your baby with formula milk from a bottle is a safe alternative to breastfeeding. All formulas are produced to guidelines that ensure they are as close to human milk as possible. Babies under the age of one should not be given cow's milk, goat's milk or condensed milk to drink. If your baby is lactose intolerant, your midwife can recommend a brand of specialised formula that is based on soya.

You can buy ready-made formula in bottles or cartons, but it is cheaper to buy it as a powder and mix it up with water. It is important to establish a routine of cleaning and sterilising the equipment you use to make up the feeds to prevent your baby getting sick. To avoid keeping your hungry baby waiting, you can keep a store of prepared formula in the fridge, but do not keep it for more than 24 hours.

It is traditional to warm a baby's bottle to body temperature, but room temperature is fine for most babies and less hassle for you if your baby will accept it. To warm a bottle, place it in a jug of hot water for a few minutes. Don't use a microwave to heat bottles as the milk may have hot spots that could scald your baby's mouth. It can also cause the nutrients to break down.

Note: Always check that the milk is warm – and not too hot – by dripping some on the inside of your wrist before feeding your baby.

Preparing

Feeding your baby

1 Hold your baby securely in your lap and make sure you give him your full attention. Do not feed a baby who is lying flat as this increases the risk of ear infections.

2 Gently touch his top lip with the teat of the bottle to make him open his mouth. Insert the teat when he is ready. If you can't see any bubbles or the teat collapses, move it gently around her mouth to let air back into the bottle.

3 Keep the bottle tilted at an angle of roughly 45 degrees so that the top of the bottle is full of formula, not air.

4 Watch your baby, talk to him in an encouraging voice and listen to his cues. Some babies want to drink the whole bottle in one go, others like to pause for air.

5 At the end of the feed, gently rub your baby's back to help him bring up wind.

Throw away any formula that hasn't been drunk after an hour.

Note: Never leave your baby alone with a propped up a bottle, as it can cause him to choke.

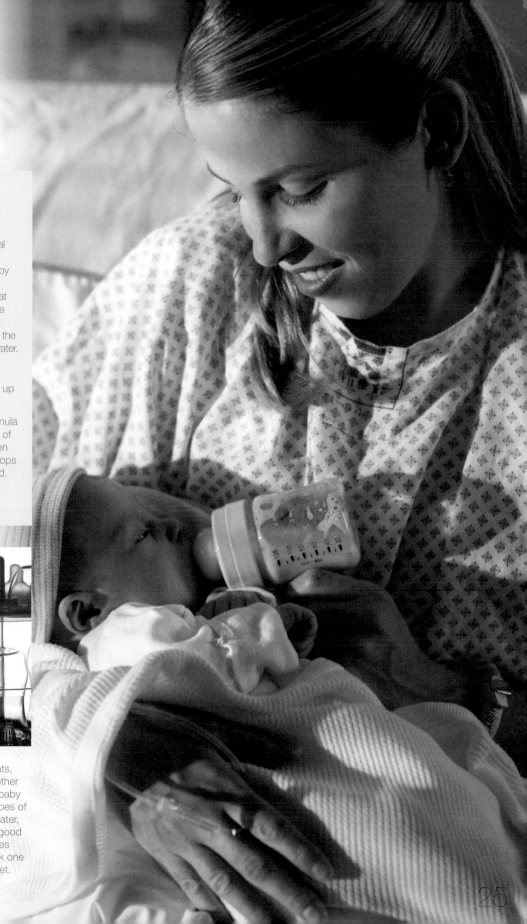

ormula

Separate the bottle into its individual
s – for example: teat, bottle and
– and wash them all in warm, soapy
er. Use a bottlebrush to clean the
les, paying attention to the thread at
top where milk can collect. Turn the
s inside out and scrub them with a
ubbing brush. Squirt water through the
's hole. Rinse everything in clean water.

Sterilise all the equipment.

Wash your hands before making up
formula.

Read the instructions on the formula
ket and add the correct amount of
led, boiled water to a bottle. Then
the correct number of level scoops
owder, using the scoop provided.

Replace the top of the bottle –
the cap – and shake to mix.

You should sterilise bottles, teats,
dummies, breast pumps and other
feeding accessories until your baby
is one. There are three main types of
steriliser on the market: cold water,
microwave and electric. It is a good
idea to look at the different types
before you buy so that you pick one
that fits your lifestyle and budget.

Changing checklist

During the first years of your baby's life, you will change a lot of nappies – up to 4,500! A newborn baby will poo several times a day and wee every one to three hours. Some babies find a wet nappy very uncomfortable, while others will happily sit for hours without complaining. However, to avoid nappy rash, you should change a nappy before or after every feed, and as soon as it is soiled.

In the UK, most babies are potty trained somewhere between the ages of two and three years old. Many children need to wear a night-time nappy for a while longer, even after they are dry during the day.

Never leave your baby unattended if they are lying on a raised surface, such as a table top or changing table.

If you are using a changing table that has no safety strap, keep one hand on your baby at all times.

Hold the nappy in place for a moment before you remove it. Babies often decide to wee as soon as a nappy is removed!

Elimination communication, or the nappy-free method, is an alternative to the conventional system of nappy-wearing and potty training. It involves listening to the signals your baby is giving and responding to them. Followers say that it is healthier and saves you money – but you have to be committed! If you are interested, look online for information or local support groups.

Always wipe a girl from front to back to help prevent infection.

Never pull back the foreskin on a boy, it takes months before it separates from the rest of his penis.

Avoid covering the umbilical stump until it has dried and fallen off.

Never try to dispose of a nappy down the toilet!

You will need:

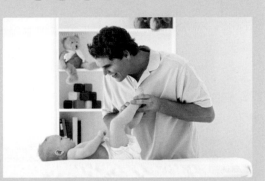

A changing table can make nappy changes easier, especially if you have had a caesarean or find it hard to bend down. It is also a good place to store all the essential baby changing items. However, if you live in a small house, you may find that it takes up precious space and opt not to buy one – or choose a design that converts to a chest of drawers for later use. As your baby gets bigger and wrigglier they will outgrow the table, and keeping them on it may become a challenge! At this point, many people switch to using a mat on the floor, where their baby will not get hurt if they roll off.

- Buy a wipe-clean changing mat or towel for your baby to lie on.

- Keep a supply of clean nappies close to your changing mat.

- Buy a roll of plastic disposal bags to put the soiled items in.

- You can use cotton wool and a bowl of boiled, cooled water to clean your baby, or baby wipes if you prefer.

- You may want a barrier cream to prevent nappy rash.

- Keep a towel or washcloth to hand to dry your baby after cleaning her.

Turn over for a step-by-step guide to changing your baby!

Never stick the tabs to your baby's skin.

The nappy should be snug, but not so tight that it pinches.

Step by step: Changing your baby's nappy

1 Make sure you have all your supplies together in one place. Wash your hands.

2 Lay your baby on the changing mat and unfasten the tabs on the dirty nappy.

3 Pull down the front half of the dirty nappy, using it to wipe the bulk of any poo from your baby.

4 Fold it over, clean side up, then lift your baby's legs in the air and slide it out from under her.

5 Place in a disposal bag.

6 Clean your baby using cotton wool and warm water, or wipes if you prefer. Lift your baby's legs, or gently roll him to one side to make sure you have cleaned thoroughly. Don't forget the creases of your baby's thighs and bottom.

7 Let your baby dry in the air for a few moments, or pat her dry with a clean cloth.

8 Apply barrier cream if necessary.

9 Unfold a fresh nappy and slide it under your baby's bottom, lifting your baby's legs by the ankles.

10 Bring the front of the nappy up between the legs, unpeel the tabs and bring the sides across to stick on the front.

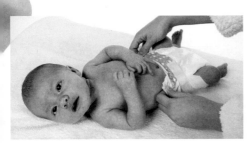

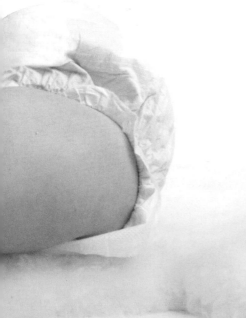

Washable nappies

There is a lot of debate around what type of nappies you should choose to use for your baby – reusable cloth nappies or disposables. As with everything, there are pros and cons for each choice. Cloth nappies have better green credentials as they do not use as many harsh chemicals, and reduce landfill. However, there are brands of 'eco' disposables that are kinder to the environment than many of the big-name brands.

Cloth nappies can be washed and reused many times. There are many different types available, from simple traditional terry squares to popper-fastened, shaped all-in-ones and pocket nappies. One advantage is that they come in all colours and styles! They can be made from a wide range of textiles including bamboo, hemp and fleece.

If you choose cloth nappies, you will also need nappy detergent to wash your nappies in, and a nappy bucket with a lid and handle to store your dirty nappies. Washable cloth nappies can be machine washed at 60°C, or you could try a local nappy laundry service.

The choice of reusable nappies can seem overwhelming at first but there are three main types.

★ Two part systems: These have a nappy to absorb wetness and an outer wrap to keep everything in.

★ All in ones: These are shaped to fit your baby. The outer wrap is attached to the absorbant inner nappy.

★ Pocket nappies: These are a pouch made from an inner layer and a waterproof outer wrap. Absorbent material is placed inside the pocket to soak up the wetness.

It is up to you to choose the type that you think will best suit your needs. There is a lot of advice available online and many companies sell a starter kit that includes all the bits and pieces you will need to get going.

Topping and tailing

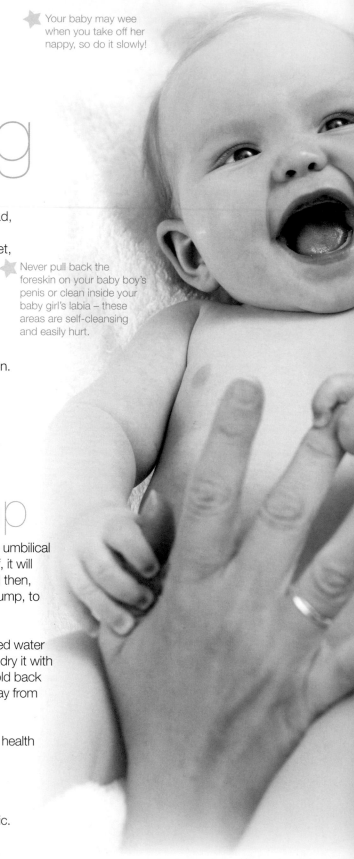

Your baby may wee when you take off her nappy, so do it slowly!

You shouldn't start bathing your baby until the stump of her umbilical cord has fallen off. Instead, keep her clean with a 'top and a tail' every day. This involves washing her face, neck, hands, feet, genitals and bottom.

You will need:

Never pull back the foreskin on your baby boy's penis or clean inside your baby girl's labia – these areas are self-cleansing and easily hurt.

- Cotton wool.
- A bowl of cooled, boiled water.
- An empty bowl for the used cotton wool .
- A towel and changing mat for your baby to lie on.
- A soft towel to dry your baby .
- A clean nappy.
- Barrier cream.

Taking care of the cord stump

It takes around 10 to 21 days for the stump of the umbilical cord to dry up and drop off. When it does drop off, it will leave a small wound that heals in a few days. Until then, you will need to clean the area around the cord stump, to prevent infection.

To do this, dip some cotton wool into cooled, boiled water and gently wipe the area around the stump. Then dry it with a new piece of cotton wool. Make sure that you fold back your baby's nappy below the stump to keep it away from any wee and to stop it rubbing.

If the area seems infected, you should talk to your health visitor or doctor. Signs of infection are:
- Pus appearing at the base of the stump.
- A bad smell coming from the stump.
- A swollen, red area around the navel.
- Your baby develops a fever or becomes lethargic.

Don't let your baby get cold. You may want to cover her body with the towel while you clean her top half, or put a vest on while you clean her bottom half.

To avoid infection, use a fresh piece of cotton wool for each part of your baby's body.

Step by Step

1 Lay your baby down on the towel – put the towel on a changing mat if you have one.

2 Clean your baby's eyes – dip a piece of cotton wool in the water and gently wipe your baby's eyes from the inner to the outer corners. Use a new piece of cotton wool for each eye.

3 Clean your baby's face – use cotton wool to wipe your baby's face, nose and ears. Do not clean inside the nose and ears. Gently pat her dry with a towel.

4 Gently unclench your baby's fists to clean her hands. Clean the creases of her arms and wipe her armpits. Pat her dry.

5 Gently clean your baby's feet and in between her toes, then pat her dry.

6 Remove her nappy and clean up any poo. Dispose of the nappy.

7 Clean her tummy and legs, making sure you clean in all the folds of skin. Pat her dry.

8 Clean your baby's genitals, then hold her ankles gently with one hand and lift her bottom in the air to clean her bottom.

Always wipe your baby girl's bottom from front to back – so that you don't transfer bacteria to her vagina.

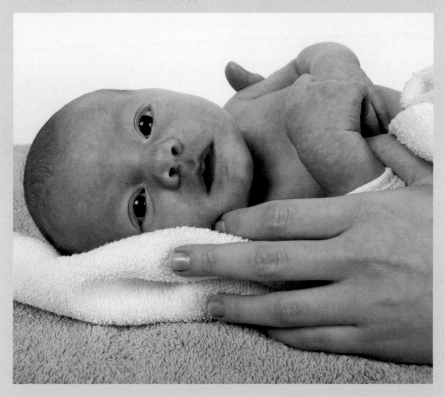

Sleep and your baby

The average baby sleeps between 16 and 20 hours a day. Although this sounds like a lot, it's not all at once and it's not all at night – which makes looking after a new baby one of the most exhausting experiences you can have!

Newborns usually sleep for about eight hours, at night, but not in one long unbroken sleep. They may sleep for just one hour, or perhaps for three or five hours before waking. Some babies like to sleep all day and are alert at night, others seem to only nap when they are being held in someone's arms – and then there are the night feeds…

It is natural to be tired, but remember there are lots of other parents in the same situation. Health visitors often suggest taking naps during the day while your baby is asleep. Try looking for support and tips from other mothers at baby groups or on the internet.

If your baby finds it hard to get to sleep, here are a few ideas that may help:

★ Try swaddling. Your health visitor or midwife can show you how to wrap your baby tightly in a blanket in a way that he will find comforting and secure.

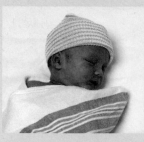

★ Put a t-shirt that has been worn by you or your partner under your baby so he is close to the warmth and smell of one of his parents.

★ Use a bouncy chair, rocker or baby seat that has gentle vibrations that will lull your baby to sleep.

★ Consider using a dummy. Some babies are very 'sucky' and will find a dummy comforting.

★ Cut down the amount of stimulation your baby is receiving. Move to a darker, quieter room and talk or sing to your baby in a hushed voice.

★ A tape recorder or toy that plays white noise – such as the sound of a hoover or a washing machine can soothe your baby with similar noises to the ones they heard in the womb.

Where to sleep?

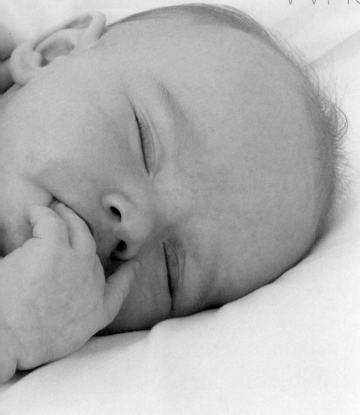

- Healthcare professionals recommend that your baby sleeps in the same room as you for the first six months – in a crib, cot or Moses basket.

- A baby room thermometer will tell you if the room is too hot or too cold – about 18° C is about right. Never place a cot next to a radiator.

- Put your baby in the 'feet to foot' position. This means that his feet should be at the bottom of the cot with a lot of empty space above his head.

- Don't let your baby overheat. Make sure he is wearing the right number of layers of clothing for the temperature and always leave his head uncovered.

- Do not smoke or allow anyone to smoke near your baby.

- Keep toys, loose bedding and pillows out of the cot.

- A baby should not have a pillow until he is over one year old.

- Never sleep with your baby on a sofa or armchair. Always put them down safely before you go to sleep.

Some parents feel that co-sleeping, or sharing a bed with their baby is more natural and makes breastfeeding easier. If you choose to co-sleep, make sure that your baby is not at risk from suffocation by your blankets, pillows or duvet. Do not share a bed with your baby if you have been drinking alcohol, or if you take drugs as you are more likely to roll onto your baby and not notice. Do not share a bed with your baby if you or your partner smoke.

SIDS (sudden infant death syndrome) or 'cot death' refers to the unexplained death of a baby younger than one year. No one knows what causes SIDS but there are ways of helping prevent it.

- Babies who sleep on their stomachs are more likely to die of SIDS, so always put your baby to sleep on their back, even for naps.

- Babies who sleep on or under soft bedding are more at risk than babies who sleep on a firm surface, so use a mattress – never pillows, quilts etc.

- Don't let anyone smoke near your baby, or share a bed with your baby if you smoke.

Dressing your baby

Dressing and undressing your newborn baby can be tricky, and on average she will need four or five changes of clothes a day. Some babies don't mind having clothes put on and taken off, but others protest loudly! Make sure that the room you are dressing your baby in is not cold, and that you are as quick and smooth with your movements as possible.

Note: If your baby really hates it when clothes go over her head, you may want to buy vests and sleepsuits that button up the front.

What to wear?

Winter
Even though the weather is cold, you must always be careful not to overdress your baby. A newborn only needs one more layer than an adult. Choose a long-sleeved vest to go under your baby's outfit and take care to protect baby's head, ears and neck with a hood or a hat.

Spring and Autumn
Dress your baby in layers that can be easily removed or added if the weather changes. Your pushchair must have a raincover to protect your baby, or if they are being carried in a sling, invest in an all-in-one waterproof suit.

Summer
If it is hot enough for you to be in short sleeves then choose short sleeves for your baby, but carry a cardigan with you just in case. Don't forget the sun cream and sun hat. You can buy a sunshade to attach to your pushchair.

Step by Step

1. Lie your baby on her back somewhere comfortable, such as on a changing mat.

2. Scrunch up the vest and stretch the neck wide so you can slip it over your baby's head in one go without touching her face.

Note: Make sure that her head is resting on your hand or the mat when you perform this movement so that it doesn't thump on the floor. Newborn babies have hardly any control over their head and neck and her head will flop back when it is not supported.

3. Next, scrunch up the sleeves and stretch out the armholes so that you can gently pull your baby's arm through.

4. Now do up the fastenings between the legs.

5. Next, lay out a sleepsuit and place your baby on top of it.

6. Gently ease her legs in, one by one then do up the fastenings. Some sleepsuits have poppers or buttons all the way down the legs, which is helpful.

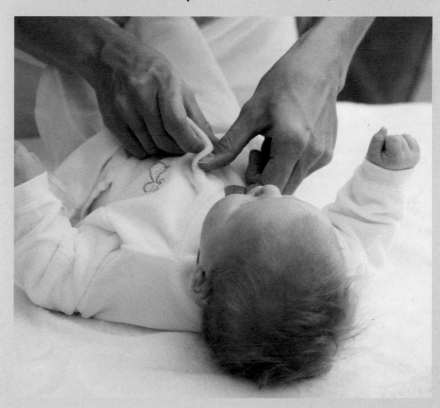

Your baby's appearance

Your newborn baby may not look exactly how you imagined. His face may be squashed from the journey through the birth canal, his skin blotchy and irritated and his head shape lopsided. Don't worry, these features are temporary and it won't take long before they fade. Here are some other features that may worry you about your newborn's appearance – but are perfectly normal.

Breasts

It's normal for both boys and girls to have swollen breasts or lumps under the nipples. This is due to exposure to maternal hormones in the womb. The same hormones that cause the mother's breasts to swell and milk glands to be stimulated can do the same to the baby's breasts. Over the weeks the tissue will shrink and become flat.

Skin

⭐ The top layer of a newborn's skin will flake off during the first week or two. This is normal and expected and doesn't require any special skin care. Peeling skin may be present at birth in some infants, particularly those who are born past their due date.

⭐ Miliaria are small, raised, red bumps that often have a white or yellow head and is often called infant acne. This is harmless and will go away within a few weeks.

⭐ Jaundice, a yellowish discolouration of the skin, can appear two or three days after the birth and will disappear in a few days. If it lasts longer, seek advice.

⭐ Some babies are born with a thin layer of downy hair over their skin called lanugo. Most of this will fall out by itself during the first few months.

Tummy

Almost all babies lose weight in the first week of life, but will gain it again in the second week and then continue to gain weight quickly.

Genitalia

Your baby's genitalia may seem large and puffy at birth, due to the effects of the mother's hormones on in the womb. Many newborn girls will have a vaginal discharge of mucus and sometimes blood for the first few days. Newborn boys may have a swollen scrotum due to a hydrocele, fluid which will disappear during the first 3 to 6 months.

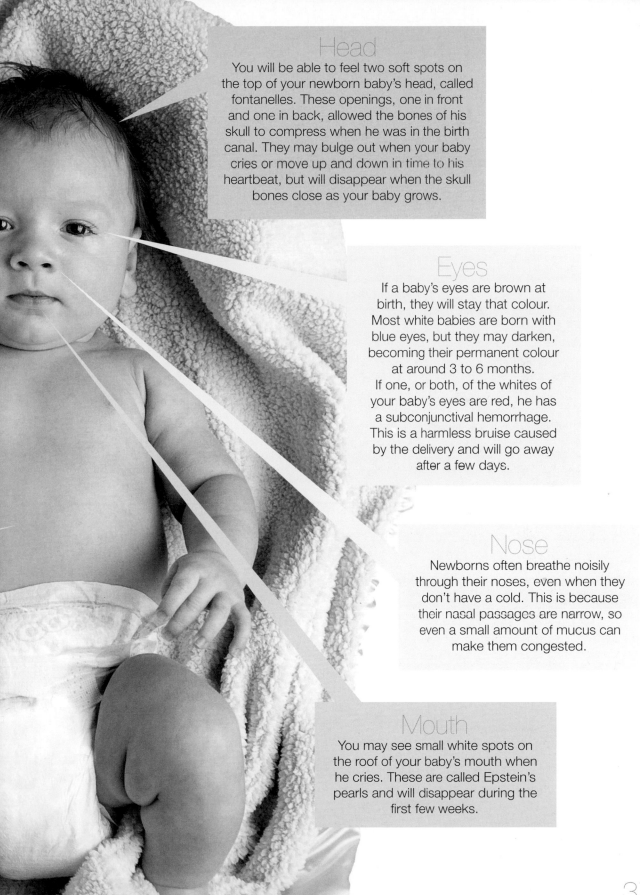

Head

You will be able to feel two soft spots on the top of your newborn baby's head, called fontanelles. These openings, one in front and one in back, allowed the bones of his skull to compress when he was in the birth canal. They may bulge out when your baby cries or move up and down in time to his heartbeat, but will disappear when the skull bones close as your baby grows.

Eyes

If a baby's eyes are brown at birth, they will stay that colour. Most white babies are born with blue eyes, but they may darken, becoming their permanent colour at around 3 to 6 months.
If one, or both, of the whites of your baby's eyes are red, he has a subconjunctival hemorrhage. This is a harmless bruise caused by the delivery and will go away after a few days.

Nose

Newborns often breathe noisily through their noses, even when they don't have a cold. This is because their nasal passages are narrow, so even a small amount of mucus can make them congested.

Mouth

You may see small white spots on the roof of your baby's mouth when he cries. These are called Epstein's pearls and will disappear during the first few weeks.

Communicating with your baby

The first few days that you spend with your baby are very important. Unless your baby was unwell after the birth, you will have been encouraged to hold her close as soon as possible, so that she recognises the smell of you and your partner, and finds comfort from your touch and warmth.

You can communicate the feelings of love you have for your baby by smiling, talking gently and giving lots of physical affection. When you hold your baby in your arms in a loving way it helps to build the bond of trust between you. Whenever you rock her, hug her and hold her close you send a nonverbal message of love that your baby understands and appreciates.

A newborn can differentiate between the sound of a human voice and other sounds and will find the familiar voice of her parents comforting. If you feel you can't think of anything to say when you are talking to your baby, try singing or cooing instead – your baby will love it.

Skin-to-skin

There is much evidence that skin-to-skin contact after the birth helps your baby in many ways. It calms both mother and baby, regulates your baby's heart rate, breathing and temperature, and stimulates her digestion. Premature babies are believed to grow and develop better if they spend some time each day in skin-to-skin contact with their mother. Try to keep up the skin-to-skin contact at times during the first few weeks of your baby's life. She will be reassured by your warmth and heartbeat.

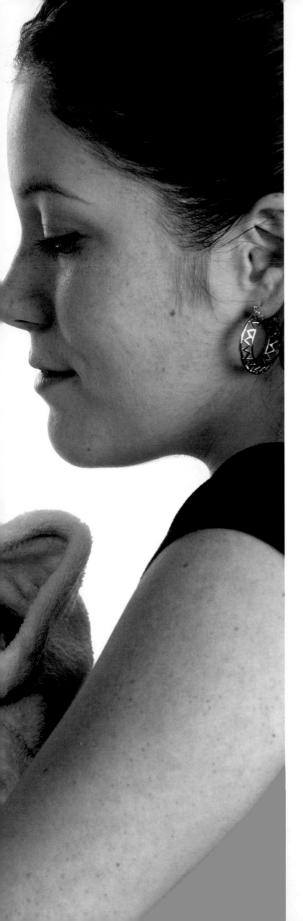

All babies cry

Crying is your baby's way of telling you what she needs. As you get to know her, you'll start to learn the difference between some of her cries, and work out what she wants. Of course she will cry if she is scared or in pain, but the chances are the reason is not that drastic! She may cry if:

★ She is hungry.
★ She wants to be held.
★ She wants to go to sleep.
★ She is too hot or too cold.
★ Her nappy is wet.

Your baby may also cry for what seems like no reason at all. She could be overstimulated by the sights and sounds of the world around her. Don't worry if you can't seem to console her straight away - crying is one way that babies shut out the world when they are feeling overwhelmed.

Keep smiling at your baby and, sometime during your newborn's first month, you may get a glimpse of a first smile back at you. This is a great addition to your baby's communication skills!

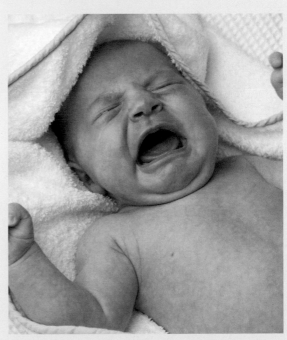

Learning about the world

Your baby will be learning a lot during the first four weeks of his life. The whole world is new, and just taking it in and trying to make sense of it is enough to tire him out. If he is sitting contentedly, don't feel that you have to jump in and shake a rattle or start 'entertaining' him. He is probably just quietly processing all the new things he is hearing and seeing. However, even a young baby can get bored or lonely. Take him with you as you move from room to room – he will like being carried in your arms or in a baby sling and will enjoy the new sounds, smells and sights from this vantage point.

Your face

Newborns prefer looking at human faces to any other pattern or colour, so make sure you give your baby lots of chances by holding him up close. Try slowly moving your head to see if his eyes follow you. Even this early, babies can recognise faces and gestures. Try putting your face close to his and sticking out your tongue to see if he mimics you.

Tummy time

Young babies spend a lot of time on their back – the safest position to sleep in – but they also need to develop and strengthen their neck muscles. The experience of being on their tummy helps babies learn to push up, roll over, sit up, crawl, and pull to a stand. So let your baby spend a short amount of tummy time regularly!

New views

Make sure that you move your baby's basket or bouncy chair to different places in the room, so that there are different things for him to look at – such as shadows on the walls, curtains moving in the wind or the branches of a tree outside the window.

Black and white

Your baby will be fascinated by black and white patterns. You can buy flashcards or books that are full of these, or even download an app if you have a smartphone. A cheaper alternative is to make your own by drawing simple black and white patterns or shapes onto card.

Baby talk

Have you found that you are using a different voice when you speak to your newborn? Most new parents (and grandparents, aunts and uncles – even complete strangers) tend to put on a high-pitched, sing-song voice and exaggerate the sounds of words to make a kind of 'baby talk'. Some people call this 'parent-ease' and it is a great way of getting your baby's attention as well as helping you to bond. So don't stop or feel self conscious, you are doing just the right thing!

41

Baby massage

Your baby is too little to play with toys, but she thrives on attention and interaction. One way to build this into your daily routine is baby massage. Many people believe that regular massage will even help your baby sleep better, help her motor skills and relieve colic. It is also a time when you can relax and concentrate on being with your baby that is separate from the 'tasks' of feeding and changing her nappy. Your baby might be unsure of what is happening the first time you try, but with daily practise will enjoy this time to bond with you.

Make sure the room is not too cold or your baby will not enjoy the experience.

Talk to your baby and maintain eye contact as you massage so that your baby feels safe and connected.

If your baby becomes irritable or upset, try massaging a different body part. If this doesn't help, stop the massage.

Keep your touch gentle at all times.

You can buy baby massage oil from health shops, or just pour a small amount of coconut, olive or sesame oil into a bowl. These won't harm your baby if they get in her mouth.

Do not massage your baby when she is hungry or directly after a feed.

Step by Step

Don't massage your baby if she has just woken up. She should be alert and able to enjoy the experience.

Remove any bangles and rings you are wearing as these may hurt your baby.

1 Remove your baby's clothes – you may choose to keep her nappy on – and place her on a towel on a changing mat.

2 Start by stroking her gently with both hands from the top of the head to the toes.

3 Using a small amount of oil, wrap your hands around her thighs – first one, then the other – and pull down in a gentle milking action.

4 Gently rotate her feet in circles to the left and right. Then stroke the top of foot, and trace circles over each sole. Gently pull each toe.

5 Repeat the milking action with each arm and rotate her wrists in each direction. Rub your thumb in tiny circles in the palm of each hand. Gently pull each finger.

6 Place both hands at the top of her chest and stroke down towards her legs.

7 Roll your baby on to her tummy and make circles down either side of her spine from neck to bottom. Do not put pressure on her spine.

8 Finish with the same brushing stroke that you started with, but this time from head to toe on her back.

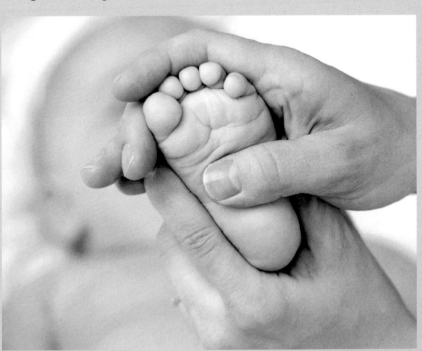

Going out with your baby

Many parents worry about taking their new baby out of the house, and in some cultures a new mother and baby are expected to stay in for a month or more. But there is no medical reason not to take your baby out, and the fresh air may do you – and the baby – good.

It's a good idea to start slowly – a walk to your local park or the shops with your baby as a first trip is fine. You might not want to go alone, so ask your partner or a friend to come with you for support. If you are taking your baby in his buggy, it is a good idea to get to know your buggy before you leave the house. Locate the brakes, learn how to use the raincover, make sure you can collapse it and put it back together again. Trying to work out all this stuff under pressure is never a good idea! If you are going to take your baby out for more than an hour or so, you'll want to make sure you're prepared for all eventualities.

Packing a baby bag

A purpose-bought changing bag will have lots of compartments so that you can find everything you need easily. It will also come with its own mini changing mat and an insulated pouch for the baby's bottle. However, a regular bag will do just as well if you are on a budget. You can buy mini changing rolls to pop in your baby bag when you are on the go. These portable mats fold up small and have pockets for wipes and nappies.

You may need:

If you are breastfeeding:
- Spare breastpads
- Nipple cream
- Scarf to cover yourself as you feed

If you are bottle feeding:
- Carton of milk
- Sterilised baby bottle
- Portable bottle warmer

For nappy changes:
- Small changing mat
- Five nappies
- Packet of wet wipes
- Nappy disposal bags
- Antibacterial hand spray – in case you can't wash your hands after a change

For you:
- Spare top – in case your baby is sick!
- Bottle of water

For baby:
- A soft toy to jingle at your baby
- Dummy
- One or two spare changes of baby clothes
- A cardigan
- Muslin squares

45

Coping with Colic

Colic is excessive crying in a baby who appears to be otherwise healthy. It affects around one in five babies and can be a distressing and frustrating experience for the parents. A baby with colic has frequent bouts of intense crying, often in the late afternoon and evening, and refuses to be comforted. Babies who draw up their legs and arch their backs while crying are usually diagnosed with colic. No one is sure what the cause of colic is, but some researchers think that indigestion or wind may play a role. Others think that colicky babies are more sensitive than others and easily overstimulated. The good news is that colic is not harmful, and there is no evidence that it has any long-term effects on a baby's health.

Talk to your doctor if you think your baby has colic, so they can rule out more serious conditions.

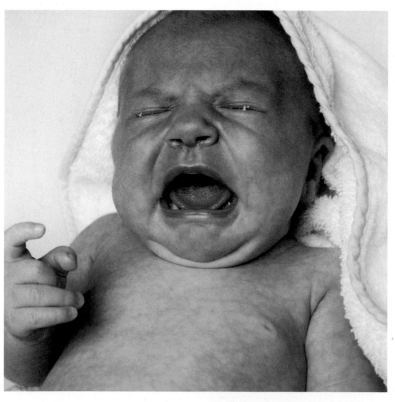

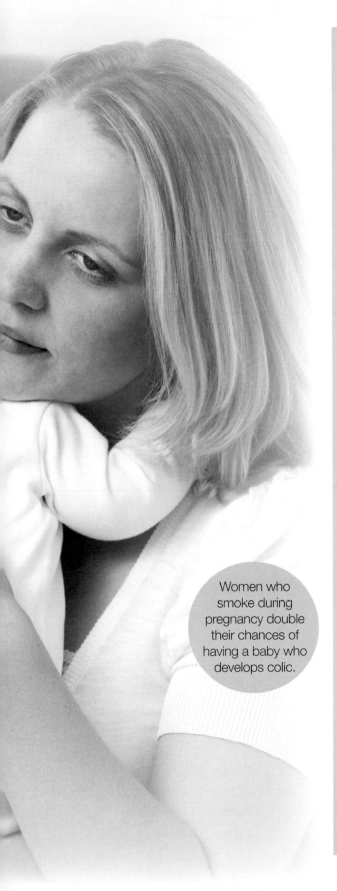

What can help?

Having to look after a baby with colic can be tough. Try to remember that it is not your fault that your baby is crying, she is not unwell and he is not rejecting you. Colic tends to peak around six weeks, then improves between three and four months and should be gone by five months.

Try these tips to see if they help your baby:
- Wrap your baby in a blanket and hold her as she cries.
- Sit your baby upright while you feed her to help stop her swallowing air.
- Always burp your baby to bring up wind after a feed.
- Cut out coffee, tea and alcohol if you are breastfeeding. Other things that it may help to avoid are cruciferous vegetables (such as cabbage and cauliflower), chocolate, dairy, soy, wheat, eggs, nuts and fish. Cut these out one by one to see if they make a difference.
- Take your baby into a quiet, dark room to cut down on stimulation.
- Push your baby around in her pram or carry her up and down the stairs.
- Let your baby listen to 'white noise' such as a vacuum cleaner or washing machine.
- Gently rub your baby's stomach or back or give her a warm bath.
- Try alternative treatments. Some parents swear by alternative treatments such as osteopathy or herbal remedies, others think there is little evidence that these are effective.

If you are bottle feeding:
- Your doctor can prescribe drops to add to your baby's bottle. The drops help release bubbles of trapped air in her digestive system.
- Use teats with larger 'fast flow' holes.
- It's possible your baby may have developed a short-term intolerance to proteins that are found in cows' milk and other dairy products. Switch formula – ask your health visitor for recommendations.

> Women who smoke during pregnancy double their chances of having a baby who develops colic.

Your body after birth

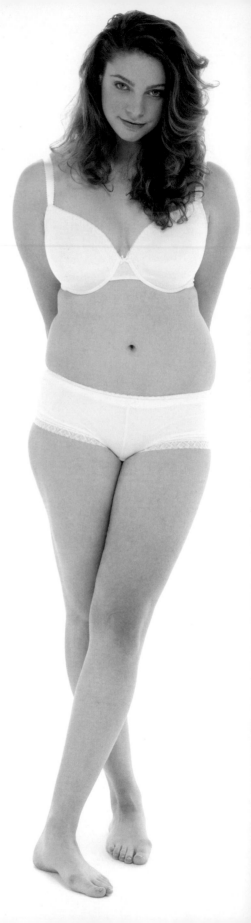

Giving birth is an amazing achievement and there are many ways you can react to it. You might feel alert, happy, satisfied, exhausted, disappointed, depressed, anxious, tired, or maybe a mixture of all of these – plus a few more for good measure! No matter what sort of labour and delivery you had, your body will be recovering from a huge upheaval and you need to allow yourself time to recover.

 After the birth you will have a bloody discharge from your vagina called lochia. This can last from several weeks, although it will get lighter after around ten days. You should use a pad, not a tampon, to soak up the blood.

 You may have afterpains as your womb shrinks back to a normal size. These feel like mild labour contractions and often happen while you are breastfeeding.

Your vagina will gradually regain much of its former tone and your pelvic floor will return to its usual position. Doing regular pelvic floor exercises will help. You may have piles, but they will soon disappear.

Small tears and grazes to your cervix, vagina and perineum will heal quickly. If it hurts to wee, it may help to do it in the shower for a while. If you had an episiostomy, this may take a while to heal. Stitches can be painful for a few days or a few weeks.

During pregnancy, hormones prevented normal hair loss. After the birth, you may find your hair starts to fall out. Don't panic – this is perfectly normal!

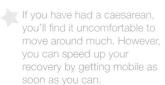 You may have stretch marks on your breasts, stomach and thighs.

If you have had a caesarean, you'll find it uncomfortable to move around much. However, you can speed up your recovery by getting mobile as soon as you can.

You won't lose all the weight you gained in pregnancy for a while, but try not to worry. Not even celebrities really 'snap back' straight away. Your body spent nine months growing your baby and it's only fair to give it the same amount of time to recover.

Six week check

Six weeks after your baby is born, you should have a postnatal check-up with your doctor. This will be a chance for you to ask questions and sort out any problems that you have. You should tell your doctor if you are finding it hard holding urine or wind, if sex is painful or if you are feeling low or depressed.

Your doctor is likely to check your blood pressure, urine and weight, examine any stitches you may have, discuss whether your periods have started, and ask if you need contraception advice. They will check that the muscles used during labour and delivery are returning to normal and the likely date of your next cervical screening test.

Nipple and breast pain

Your nipples may be sensitive after birth and while breastfeeding, but if they are very sore, this can mean that something is wrong and you should talk to your health visitor or a doctor. Some common problems include thrush, dermatitis, bacterial infection or eczema. You may also feel a lump in your breast, which is caused by milk getting into your breast tissue instead of your milk ducts.

If areas of your breasts are red, hard, sore, hot or swollen, and you have flu-like symptoms such as chills, headache, high temperature you may have mastitis. Don't stop feeding as this can make it worse, and do see your doctor who will be able to help and may prescribe antibiotics.

Mood swings and baby blues

A new baby brings huge changes to your life and all new parents need to go through a period of adjustment. How you handle this new phase of life varies dramatically from person to person. Some find that the period of adjustment is temporary, others find that it takes a long time and can cause distress.

Spending time alone with a new baby can lead to feelings of isolation. Get out of the house and go for walks, and keep talking to your friends and your partner.

Try to establish a basic routine for your day, such as a bath in the evenings or a walk in the mornings. This will help you feel more in control.

Baby Blues

During the first week after birth, many mothers feel sensitive, irritable and prone to crying. These feelings tend to peak three days after the birth and are caused by hormonal changes after childbirth. Ask your partner or friend to make you meals, help you organise your time and get some rest. Don't feel embarrassed about needing to talk things through or cry. These feelings will usually go away after a few days.

Anxiety and depression

Postnatal depression usually develops in the first four to six weeks after childbirth, although in some cases it may not develop for several months. There are many symptoms, such as feeling constantly down and unable to cope, but many women are not aware they have the condition. A doctor may use these questions to diagnose postnatal depression:

1. During the past month, have you often been bothered by feeling down, depressed or hopeless?

2. During the past month, have you often been bothered by taking little or no pleasure in doing things that normally make you happy?

If you answer yes to one question, it is possible that you have postnatal depression. If you answer yes to both, it is probable.

Note: If you think you are experiencing anxiety or are worried about postnatal depression, you should talk to your health visitor or doctor who will be able to offer help and support, such as antidepressants or counselling.

★ If you find yourself feeling overwhelmed try to make time for yourself each day – even as little as 20 minutes in the bath, reading a book, or having a nap on your own can make a difference. It may seem impossible but with a little planning it can happen.

 Never say 'no' to help. You and your partner may want to draw up a list of chores and divide them up between you. If a friend or relative asks if they can help, give them a specific task such as the washing up or hanging out baby clothes to dry.

★ You may find yourself the recipient of a torrent of advice from other well-meaning mothers. Remember that there is more than one way of bringing up a baby, and what suits someone else's baby might not work for you. Listen to the advice and talk it over with your partner, friend or health visitor before deciding what to do.

Sex after birth

Some people think that you should wait until the six-week check before having sex, but really there is no problem with having sex sooner, if you and your partner feel that it's the right time. Some couples restart their sex life in the first four weeks after birth, others wait for months. Every couple is different and you should not feel pressured into having sex before you are ready.

It is a good idea to let wounds heal and stitches dissolve before you start. Even if you haven't had an episiotomy or tear, the area can feel bruised and sensitive for a while. Some women feel uncomfortable about their body after birth, or are just too tired to think about sex. If this is the case, let your partner know how you feel and make sure that you continue spending time being affectionate together.

Note: Even if your periods have not started, you can still get pregnant. Talk to your doctor about contraceptive advice.

1 Month+

Your baby's development

The first six months of your baby's life takes her from a sleepy newborn to a wide-eyed adventurer who wants to touch, taste, feel and look at all the things in the world around her. Don't forget that as your baby grows, you are growing as a parent too. By the time she is learning to sit up, you'll be an expert at nappy changing, buggy folding, milk feeding and the hundred other things that having a baby has brought into your life – including multi-tasking and getting by on a lot less sleep!

By four months, your baby is likely to have doubled her birth weight. Her eyes might be starting to change colour around now too.

It takes a while for babies to be able to regulate their body temperature, and up to three months for their circulation to adapt to life outside the womb. This means that it's normal for your baby's fingers and toes to feel cold when you touch them, but don't forget to cover them up with gloves and socks if the weather is cold outside.

One month

Your baby will begin to smile and respond to the sounds around her. She will lift her head if you lie her on her tummy as if she's doing a press-up. She may start to notice that her hands and feet belong to her and enjoy playing with them!

Two months

Your baby will love colourful mobiles and toys dangling above her. Her arm and leg movements are becoming smoother and she may try to bat at things with her fists. She has a tight grip, but is not able to let go yet – so watch out for your hair!

Three months

Your baby will be able to sleep for longer stretches of time and her daytime sleep schedule is becoming more of a routine, with a few naps that last for around 1-2 hours each. She may have learnt to roll from her tummy to her back, so don't leave her unattended on high surfaces!

Four months

Your baby will learn to sit and start to explore the world around her, reaching out for objects, looking at textures, patterns and colours and putting anything she finds in her mouth. She will be cooing and babbling words such as 'dadadada' and 'mamamam'.

Five months

Your baby may be able to sit up for a short time without assistance, and will enjoy strengthening her legs by bouncing up and down on your thighs when you sit. She can blow raspberries and make bubbles and can recognize her name when you call her.

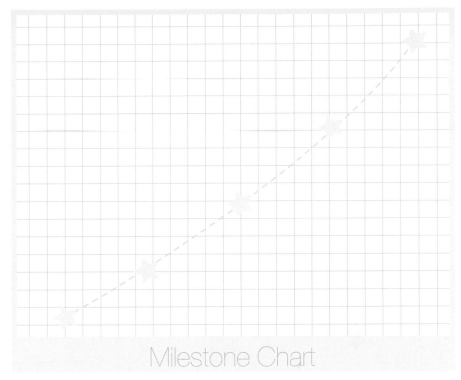

Your baby
will lift objects
up and suck
them

Your baby
will start to make
new and different
sounds

Your baby will
reach out for
objects

Your baby will
lift her head

Your baby will
start to smile

Milestone Chart

4-6 weeks   6-12 weeks   3-5 months   4-6 months   5 months

Some studies have shown
that in the first months after giving
birth, parts of a mother's brain may
grow – the parts involved in motivation,
reward behaviour and emotion
regulation. This could show that
the brain reshapes itself to motivate
her to take care of her baby
and feel happy and rewarded
when she does.

Feeding in public
Breastfeeding

While you are getting used to it, you may prefer to feed your baby at home. But as you get more confident, you will be able to feed him when you are out and about. You shouldn't ever be made to feel uncomfortable about breastfeeding in public. It is illegal in the UK for anyone to ask a breastfeeding woman to leave a public place such as a café, shop or public transport.

Before you go out, think of places you will be comfortable breastfeeding, such as a café that is breastfeeding friendly or a secluded spot in a park. Most shopping centres and many baby shops and larger department stores have a room with a chair set aside for breastfeeding. Avoid public loos – they are not hygienic places to feed a baby. If you are desperate for privacy, you could always ask to use a changing room in a clothes shop. Some mothers like to wear loose tops that they can lift up to feed, others prefer stretchy tops that they can pull down, keeping their tummy covered. Many like to cover their chests with a scarf or muslin as they feed.

Warming a bottle out and about

Most coffee shops will help you warm a baby bottle. Some give you a cup of boiling water, others will take the bottle and warm it for you. You can also buy portable bottle warmers to take with you – some are a thermos flask with a beaker to stand your bottle in, others are warm pads that wrap round the bottle.

If you are not going to be out for long, you can put very hot water in the bottle and keep it in a thermal bag. Make sure that the water is not too hot before you mix it with the powder! If you are out in the car, you can buy bottle warmers that plug into the cigarette lighter.

Bathing your baby

Bathing a baby for the first time can be scary! It takes a bit of practice to feel confident handling a slippery, wet baby and it's a good idea to have someone on hand to help you the first few times you do it.

It's up to you how often you bath your baby. Babies only need a bath two or three times a week, but a daily bath can be a gentle introduction to a soothing bedtime routine. Most babies love the water and find bathtime a fun, bonding experience.

If your baby seems scared of the water, try getting into the bath together. It is easier to do this if someone else holds the baby while you get in and out! If you are not bathing your baby every day, make sure you regularly wash their face, genitals and bottom.

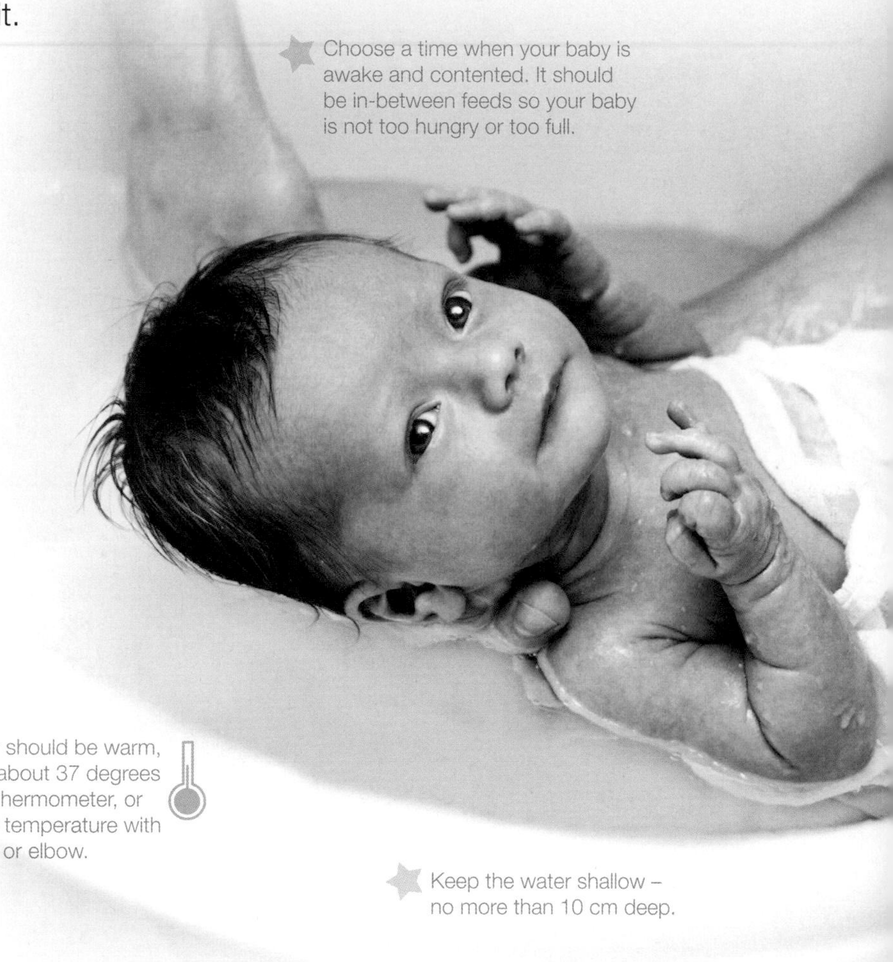

Make sure the room is warm and that you have everything you need at hand.

Choose a time when your baby is awake and contented. It should be in-between feeds so your baby is not too hungry or too full.

The water should be warm, not hot – about 37 degrees C. Use a thermometer, or check the temperature with your wrist or elbow.

Keep the water shallow – no more than 10 cm deep.

Bathtime checklist:

★ A baby bath is not essential, but many people find it makes bathtime easier. You can use a baby bath inside your bathtub or put it on the floor on a towel.

★ A bath support will keep your baby secure in the tub.

★ A plastic bath mat stops babies from slipping.

★ A soft flannel or sponge is ideal for a newborn's delicate skin.

★ Use cotton wool to clean your newborn baby's face.

★ A soft bath towel with a hood helps to keep your baby warm after the bath.

★ A baby bath thermometer will tell you if the water is too hot or cold.

Mix the water well to make sure there are no hot patches.

Step by Step

1 Make sure you have all your bath supplies ready. Lay out a clean nappy and change of clothes for your baby to change into.

5 Use your hand to scoop warm water over her body throughout the bath to keep him warm.

6 Wash your baby from top to bottom, front and back with your hand or a flannel. Then use a flannel to gently wash her scalp.

7 It is a good idea to use moistened cotton wool balls to carefully clean your baby's face and eyes.

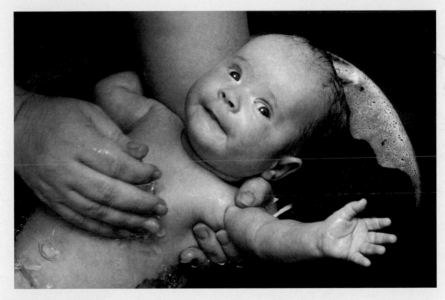

2 Fill the tub with shallow, warm water.

3 Bring your baby to the bath and undress him. Keep talking to her in a calm voice, explaining what you are doing. She can't understand the words but she will find the tone reassuring.

4 Slowly slip your baby into the tub, feet first. Use your hand to support her neck and head and keep them out of the water.

8 Don't use baby wash or soap on her face.

9 Rinse your baby with handfuls of water and wipe her down with the flannel.

10 Lift her out of the bath with one hand supporting her neck and head and the other supporting her bottom.

11 Wrap your baby in a hooded towel and gently pat her dry.

Never leave your baby unattended. A baby can drown in less than an inch of water and in less than a minute. If you must answer the phone or doorbell, take your baby with you, wrapped in a towel.

★ You will need a mild wash and shampoo designed for babies' sensitive skin and hair.

★ After the bath is a great time to massage your baby with oil that will help keep their skin soft and supple.

Helping your baby to sleep

Until his weight gain is established, usually in the first few weeks of his life, your newborn baby will sleep most of the day and night and should be woken up every three or four hours to feed. At around the age of three months, his sleep time will start to shift towards night. This is the age when many babies will start 'sleeping through' – or going for five or six hours in a row without waking. If your baby is finding it hard to sleep in longer chunks, these suggestions may help.

If another mother tells you that her baby is sleeping 'through the night' it is a good idea to ask her, politely, to define what this phrase means to her. The chances are, it's not going to mean what you would have considered to be a full night's sleep before you had a baby. Remember, all babies are different.

Falling asleep alone

Don't let your baby fall asleep while he is feeding or being rocked as he will naturally come to associate these things with going back to sleep, and want them in the middle of the night when he wakes. It may be tricky at first, but aim to put your baby in his cot when he is drowsy, but before he has fallen asleep. Babies who fall asleep on their own will find it easier to go back to sleep when they wake in the night.

Day and night

Make a distinction between the way you act around your baby in the day and the way you act in the night. He needs to get used to the idea that night is a time for quiet and sleep. Keep any interaction to a minimum when you go to him in the night, and speak in a soft voice. Don't make direct eye contact, but don't look away from him, as he may find this distressing – keep your eyes on his stomach. Avoid changing his nappy unless you really have to.

Light and dark

Darkness will trigger your baby's brain to release melatonin, a hormone which aids sleep. Keep the light dim in your baby's bedroom and the other rooms you are in before bedtime. Lower the lights an hour or so before bedtime to help him sense that night is on its way. Try to avoid leaving a nightlight on in his room. If the room is very bright in the summer, invest in blackout blinds or curtains. You can buy ones that stick onto the window with suction pads if you don't want to fit them. If your baby wakes up in the night, don't turn on the lights or take him into a bright room. By keeping everything dark and not leaving the room, you are reinforcing the message that this is not the daytime.

Stay away

If you find yourself jumping every time you hear a sound on the baby monitor, you might want to think before you rush in. Babies often cough and cry in their sleep, and will carry on sleeping if they are not picked up – although this is bound to wake them. Try leaving your baby for a short while to see if he settles himself before you go to him.

Note: Never leave your baby for a long time, or if you can hear that he is distressed.

Teething troubles

The age at which the first tooth appears differs from child to child, although the complete set of 20 baby teeth (or milk teeth) is usually present by the age of two-and-a-half. The first adult teeth appear at around six years of age. Your baby's teeth will appear when they are ready and if your baby is an early or late starter this is not an indication of ill-health.

Early signs of teething include:
- Chewing on solid objects.
- Dribbling.
- Irritability.
- Loss of appetite.
- Swollen gums.
- Trouble sleeping.

Most doctors say that teething doesn't cause fever or runny noses or diarrhoea or bad nappy rash – these are all myths.

Brush your baby's teeth as soon as they appear, using a soft brush with a small head. You will only need a small smear of baby toothpaste that contains fluoride. It can be easier to cradle your baby and brush their teeth from behind, as if you were brushing your own.

Rub your baby's gums with a clean finger to help ease the pressure on his gums.

If your baby is dribbling a lot, he can wear soft bibs throughout the day to prevent irritation to his skin. Place a muslin under his head while he is asleep to keep him dry.

If your baby is very irritable and has trouble sleeping, talk to your doctor or health visitor. They may suggest using baby ibuprofen to ease the pain.

Your baby's teeth

The average order of appearance of a baby's teeth:

- 6 months – two lower central incisors, followed by two upper central incisors.
- 7 months – four central incisors
- 8 months – four side incisors
- 10-14 months – four back molars
- 16-20 months – four canines
- 24-30 months – four more back molars

A teething ring made from firm rubber will help your baby. Some are filled with gel that can be put in the fridge.

You can buy teething gels over the counter from your pharmacist which contain a small amount of local anaesthetic and are applied onto your baby's gums.

Never give your baby ice to hold against his gums or put a teething ring in the freezer. This could cause burns.

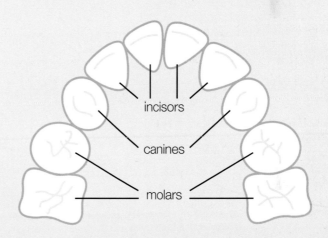

incisors

canines

molars

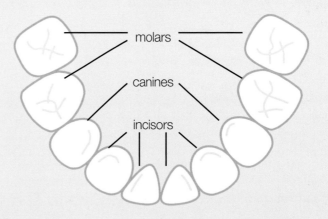

molars

canines

incisors

Your baby's vaccinations

Many parents dread taking their baby to be vaccinated. They worry that a cocktail of vaccines will be too much for such a tiny person, or think that in the modern world, with better access to health care and nutrition your baby should be able to cope naturally with disease. However, the scientific evidence is on the side of vaccinating your baby. Childhood diseases such as mumps, measles and polio were a huge threat to children before recent immunisation programmes largely wiped them out – and it wouldn't take much of a fall in immunisation levels for epidemics to flare up again. Medical opinion is that the benefits far outweigh the risks. If you are worried about vaccinating your child, you should talk to your doctor who will be able to discuss your concerns.

Vaccinations, MMR and autism

Some groups believe thimerosal, a preservative used in vaccines, is toxic to the central nervous system and linked to autism in children. However, a number of studies have reviewed the evidence and concluded there is no link. British medical journal The Lancet published a study in 1998 that connected the MMR vaccine with autism. The study was later repudiated by several of the researchers and retracted by The Lancet.

Note: Thimerosal has never been used in the MMR vaccine, but people often confuse the two issues.

Vaccines for young children (offered for free to everyone in the UK):

2 months:
- 5-in-1 (first dose) (DTaP/IPV/Hib). This single jab contains vaccines to protect against five separate diseases - diphtheria, tetanus, pertussis (whooping cough), polio and Haemophilus influenzae type b (Hib, a bacterial infection that can cause severe pneumonia or meningitis in young children).
- Pneumococcal infection

3 months:
- 5-in-1 (second dose)(DTaP/IPV/Hib)
- Meningitis C

4 months:
- 5-in-1 (third dose) (DTaP/IPV/Hib)
- Pneumococcal infection, second dose
- Meningitis C, second dose

Between 12 and 13 months:
- Hib/Men C booster. Given as a single jab containing meningitis C, third dose and Hib, fourth dose.
- MMR (measles, mumps and rubella), given as a single jab
- Pneumococcal infection, third dose

3 years and 4 months:
- MMR second jab
- 4-in-1 pre-school booster (DtaP/IPV). Given as a single jab containing vaccines against diphtheria, tetanus, pertussis and polio.

After the jab

All babies are different and it's hard to predict how your baby will react to a vaccination. Some babies cry for a short while, others for longer. Some go straight to sleep, some get a slight temperature. He is likely to have a sore lump where the needle went in. If your baby seems very distressed, you can give him Calpol (baby paracetamol) by squirting it into his mouth with a syringe. Always read the label for the correct dosage. Some babies have a reaction that is similar to the onset of the disease, such as a fever and cough that appears several days after the injection.

Your baby's senses

It will be a while before she can talk, but your baby still needs to communicate her needs and feelings to you. You will find that you learn to pick up on your baby's cues and signals fast and can quickly tell if she is unhappy or anxious. For example, if your baby is overstimulated, you will notice the way that she fusses and finds it hard to go to sleep, jerks her arms and legs around and avoids looking at your face. This is your cue to take her into a quieter room, to rock her and soothe her. It is important to respond to your baby's cues to help your baby feel secure. Studies have shown that parents' responsiveness to their baby's signals can affect her social and cognitive development.

Touch

Your baby will enjoy being held firmly and closely by you. Many babies enjoy to be lightly stroked or massaged, although often not until they are more than a few weeks old. Loving touch is a way to help you and your baby bond, creating strong ties between you. This bond is your baby's first model for relationships and gives her a sense of security and self-esteem.

Smell

At birth, your baby's sense of smell is good enough for her to be able to use it to identify her parents. Try to avoid wearing perfume and aftershave while your baby is young as she will be reassured by the familiar smell of your skin. Your baby may be sensitive to strong smells, so it is a good idea to avoid using perfumed toiletries on your baby and to be aware that if she seems unhappy, she may be bothered by a strong cooking or cleaning smell that you may not have registered.

Hearing

Your newborn has been hearing sounds since she was in the womb. This is why the sound of your heartbeat, or white noise, will calm her down. Your baby may be startled by sudden, loud noises such as the doorbell, or a dog barking, but her favourite sounds will be the sounds of her parents' voices when you talk to her in loving tones.

Note: Babies will have a hearing check during their first few weeks, as hearing loss can occur in up to two babies in every 1,000. Most often, this can be treated and the hearing restored.

Non-verbal cues

⭐ Rubbing her eyes and ears – in many babies this is a clear signal that they are tired. Your baby may find pulling her ear comforting.

⭐ Rooting – even after the rooting reflex has faded, your baby may still bob up and down on your arm or shoulder is she is hungry.

⭐ Turning her head away – this may mean that she is overstimulated and needs a short break from eye contact. Give her some time and wait until she turns back to you.

⭐ Squirming and arching her back – this could signal that a young baby has reflux or that your baby has had enough to eat. At four months it may mean that she is trying to roll over. Change your baby's position – pick her up if she is lying down, or lie her down somewhere safe and comfortable is she is being held.

Sight

Your baby is senstive to movement, and may find any sudden gestures and movements alarming. She will pick up on your body language if you are stressed, and hurrying around, and you may find that she becomes fretful at just the moments when you don't have the time to stop and hug her. This is why, if you are searching for your house keys so that you can leave the house, you may find the situation is suddenly worsened by a crying baby. It's worth taking time to stop and talk to her calmly before you carry on your search!

Speech

Long before she can speak clearly, your baby can understand the tone of your voice. This is why it is important to smile at your baby as you talk to her and keep your tone upbeat, warm and loving. Between one and three months, your baby will smile, laugh or get excited when you talk to them and will start to make cooing and gurgling noises back at you. Look at her while you talk and listen to her when she coos and babbles back at you. In time, she will start to imitate your facial expression and learn how this relates to the meaning of the words you are saying. She will work out that conversations happen when people take turns, and you can help her with this by imitating the sounds that she makes back to you. She says 'ba ba!' You smile at her, and say encouragingly 'ba ba!' then wait for her to make her next move.

Learning to crawl

Between six and ten months old, your baby will be ready to get around. You may see him getting up on all fours and rocking backwards and forwards and think he's about to go… then he collapses down onto his stomach again! Don't worry, it just takes time. Learning to crawl is a complicated process. Your baby has to have enough strength in his arms, shoulders and legs, and needs to work out how to coordinate his arms and legs so that they work together. Babies often start by crawling backwards because their arms are stronger than their legs at first. They lift up their arms, push off – and end up further away from their destination!

Before your baby can get going, he has to lose some of his infant reflexes and gain new ones. The startle and the grasping reflex would hinder his ability to crawl, so they fade during the first year of life. Two new reflexes, the lateral tilt and the parachuting reflex, make your baby extend a hand to steady himself if he wobbles and to reach up and grab at something if he falls.

Other ways your baby might get around:

* Rolling over and over to get to where he wants to be.

* Lying on his stomach and pulling himself forward like a commando.

* Bending one knee and extending the opposite leg to scoot forward.

* Shuffling on his bottom.

Don't worry if your baby isn't learning to crawl at the same speed as your friends' children. Some babies are more interested in learning to talk, or go straight to walking without crawling at all. There's no proof that skipping the crawling stage will cause problems further down the line. If your baby reaches 12 months and hasn't shown that he can move his arms and legs together in a coordinated motion, or shown any interest in moving around, (including rolling and bottom shuffling) you can talk to your doctor.

Helping your baby

⭐ Make sure that your baby is having regular, supervised amounts of time on his stomach to help him strengthen his muscles. If he doesn't like being on his stomach, try to make it fun by putting interesting toys in front of him, just out of reach. Give him lots of encouragement.

⭐ When your baby can move, set up an obstacle course with pillows and cushions and try it out together. This is a fun game for both of you and will help him improve his speed and agility.

⭐ Once your baby has started crawling, let him crawl around the floor as much as he likes. It's good exercise and will tire him out – he might even start eating more and sleeping better as a consequence.

⭐ Don't let your baby try climbing stairs for a while, as this could be dangerous. Always supervise him on the stairs, even when he is more confident.

⭐ If your baby can crawl or pull himself up to standing, remove any toys or cot bumpers from his cot so that he does not climb on them and fall out.

⭐ Special 'crawling shoes' are available, but not essential. There is no need for outdoor shoes until your baby is walking confidently. Let him go barefoot around the house as this will help to strengthen the arches of his feet and his leg muscles.

Note: Before your baby starts to crawl, make sure your house is safe for him to move around in. Put stair gates at the top and bottom of the stairs.

Games to play with your baby

From the moment she is born, your baby is interested in the world around her. Although she will not be able to play the sorts of games that older children do, she will still be able to enjoy simple games that allow her to spend crucial time bonding with you. Singing songs, hugging and talking to her are all stimulating activities for a young baby and will bring your closer together. As she grows older, you can incorporate some more fun games into your daily routine.

Your baby's attention span will vary depending on her age, mood or even the time of day. You will be able to tell if your baby is not enjoying a game, as she will turn away or cry. Leave the game for a few days and come back to it – she may enjoy it another time. If she seems to be getting restless and overstimulated, stop what you are doing and switch to a calmer activity.

One month

Your baby will love looking at your face, so hold her close and let her look. Now try sticking your tongue out slowly and putting it back again. Do this for a while and the chances are your baby will copy you. Babies love to imitate – it's how they learn! Now wrinkle your nose, wiggle your eyebrows and try getting her to copy your smile.

Two months

Your baby's sense of hearing is well-developed, and introducing her to a wide variety of sounds can be a fun game. Collect together noisy objects, such as a squeaky toy, a rattle, waxed paper to scrunch up, or spoons to clack together, then sit or lie next to your baby and demonstrate them, one by one.

Three months

Try playing with a floaty scarf. Wave it in front of your baby's face, drape it over her head and take it off again, or hide behind it and blow it to make it move. She will be fascinated to watch you. Play 'peekaboo' by popping out from behind the scarf and giving your baby a big smile.

Four months

Lie on your back and bring your knees up to your chest. Then balance your baby on your shins, keeping hold of her hands and rock her gently side to side and backwards and forwards. Keep smiling to reassure her and show what fun you are having, and make 'zoom' noises. She should find this a lot of fun – but don't go too fast, and stop if she seems anxious.

Five months

Buy a bottle of cheap bubble mix, put your baby in her high chair and blow bubbles! She will love watching them float down and may try to pop them herself. Try blowing them from different directions, high and low, to give her a gentle surprise. Laugh and talk to her in between blows, congratulating her if she catches any.

Baby groups

It shouldn't be hard for you to find a baby group near you. Have a look online, or in local magazines and newspapers. Look at notice boards in libraries, community centres or local churches – many groups are in church halls, but that doesn't mean that they will be religious, although some may be.

Going to a baby group may seem a daunting prospect at first, but it's definitely worth a try. You may want to go to a group a few times to see if it is right for you – after you've been regularly for a few weeks, your face will become familiar and people may start to open up. But don't feel bad about trying a different one if you feel that you don't belong there.

If you are too shy to keep starting up conversations, you may prefer to find a group that is focused on an activity – such as baby massage or yoga. Doing a group activity makes it easier to talk to other people. But there are lots of good reasons for giving a baby group a go:

- It is cheap – often groups ask for a small donation to cover the cost of a cup of tea and biscuits, but it is unlikely to be much.

- It is good to get out of the house with your baby – and the park is a less tempting option during the winter months.

- You can meet new people, talk to other mothers and maybe find new friends.

- You will always find someone who is genuinely interested in talking about your lack of sleep, feeding problems, nappy changing disasters…

- When your child is older, he will enjoy the different toys, books and activities on offer. There may also be a chance for 'messy play' such as painting or craft that you might not want to do at home. He will also get a chance to socialise with other children.

Hints and tips for baby group survival:

★ Don't have preconceived ideas about who you will get on with. Smile at everyone!

★ Remember that the other parents are more likely to be shy, sleep-deprived or just having a bad day than aloof, superior and judging you.

★ Some parents will know each other well and go to the groups as a group. They may welcome you, or not want to meet new people. If it is the latter, there will be plenty of other people to talk to.

★ You don't have to talk about your babies, although it is a good start. Some parents may be really happy not to talk about them for a change or welcome the chance to talk about their jobs and last night's television.

Ways to start a conversation

★ Just smile and say hello
★ Mention the weather
★ Ask which is the other parent's child (if it's not obvious!)
★ Praise the other parent's child's looks / clothes / behaviour
★ Confide that this is the first time you have been to this group

Childcare options

If you are planning to go back to work, you should make sure that you don't leave your childcare planning until the last minute. It may take you a while to find the option that is right for you – and many nurseries and childminders have waiting lists.

You need to find somewhere that works for your baby and fits into your lifestyle. If you are lucky enough to have family or friends who are close to your child and happy to look after her, then this is the cheapest and most flexible option – although if money is involved in the arrangement, the carer needs to be registered with Ofsted and will have to complete a CRB check and an inspection. If this is not available to you, there are four main choices.

Day nursery

Day nurseries follow the early years foundation stage (EYFS) which sets out a structure of care and learning. You can expect your child to take part in painting, imaginative play, story time, building blocks, puzzles, dancing, singing and music time, cooking and dressing up. One benefit of a day nursery is that your child will learn how to develop her social skills and learn to be part of a group, which will help when she starts school. If you choose a nursery that is close to her prospective school, it is likely she will have friends starting in the same year as her, which will be reassuring.

Try to visit a few nurseries to get a feel for what you like and don't like. Other than cost, you may want to know how flexible the nursery is about sessions, if they have an outdoor area or take the children for regular visits to a park, whether meals and nappies are provided, and how high the turnover of staff is. Ask to see the latest Ofsted report for the nursery, which will show you how the nursery has been graded after an inspection.

Nanny

A nanny should have a childcare qualification and a certain amount of experience caring for children, and will look after your child in your home on a one-to-one basis. You will have an employment contract and pay a salary as well as making tax and NI arrangements. (If you use an agency, they will help with these arrangements.) A nanny is one of the more expensive childcare options, although you could look for a nanny-share with a friend. A live-in nanny will cost more than a day nanny. You should do a background check before hiring a nanny, unless an agency has done this for you. You will want to see her ID, driving licence, childcare qualifications, first aid certificate, CRB check, Ofsted registrations and references. It is important that you get on with your nanny, that you trust her and that you have the same approach to childcare. You should prepare a list of questions to ask her at the interview. For example:

- How flexible is she about holidays?
- Does she expect to cook, clean and do housework as part of her job?
- What would her plan be for a typical day – both outside and in the home?
- How does she deal with tantrums?
- What does she enjoy most about her job?

Childminder

A childminder will look after your child in their home – many are parents and look after their own child at the same time. A childminder can look after up to six children younger than eight, as long as no more than three of them are under the age of five. As your child gets older, a childminder will usually be flexible enough to pick her up from pre-school, or school and look after him until you return from work, or even in the school holidays. When picking a childminder, it's a good idea to talk to other mothers who use them, and to check the latest Ofsted report. Ask about the childminder's daily routine and the types of activity on offer. Childminders must have a CRB check and have completed first aid training as well a course that covers nutrition, hygiene and health and safety.

Au Pair

An au-pair will help part-time with childcare and housework in return for free accommodation and food. You would usually expect a girl aged between 17 and 27 who is studying in this country. She will not be able to provide solo care for a baby under the age of 2 and will need most of her evenings free for studying or socialising. An au-pair can stay with a family over the summer, for six months or a year. You should always source an au-pair from an agency or do your own background check before you employ her. It is important that you find someone you get on well with, who can fit into your routine without causing a problem.

Exercising with your baby

When you've just had a baby, finding the time to exercise can seem impossible. Not only do you have to do it with your child in tow – or find someone to look after her – but the lack of sleep and breastfeeding can leave you drained and unmotivated. However, finding time for gentle exercise can help lift your mood and your energy levels as well as help your body recover from pregnancy and birth.

If you exercised throughout your pregnancy and had a normal vaginal delivery, you can safely start light exercise, such as walking and stretching, within days of giving birth. If you weren't very active during your pregnancy or had a caesarean you should check with your doctor first. This can be done at the six-week check, and many mother and baby exercise classes ask you to wait for this before you join.

Note: It's important not to overdo it. Remember that your joints and ligaments will still be loose for three to five months after giving birth. Most women develop a gap in their abdominal muscles during pregnancy, which takes between four and eight weeks to close up.

Pelvic floor exercises

Your pelvic floor supports your bladder, bowel and womb. Having a weak pelvic floor means that you find yourself leaking a little urine when you cough, sneeze or exercise. This is called stress incontinence and it affects a third of new mothers. Pelvic floor exercises are simple, cheap and effective, and you can do them anywhere! They will help your perineum and vagina heal more quickly and stop the accidental urine leaks. For the first few days after giving birth, you may not be able to feel your pelvic floor muscles working. This is because the nerves have been stretched and the feeling will come back soon.

Step by Step

1 Find your pelvic floor muscles. Try to tighten and lift up the muscles around your vagina and back passage – imagine that you are trying to stop the flow of urine when you're on the toilet. If you put a couple of fingers into your vagina, when doing the exercise you should feel a gentle squeeze.

2 The correct movement is upwards and inwards, not bearing down. Your stomach, thighs and buttocks should not move while you're doing the exercise as this is exercising the wrong muscle groups. Don't hold your breath!

3 You should do slow and fast contractions. Slow contractions help the strength of your pelvic floor and fast contractions help it to cope with pressure.

Slow
Lift your pelvic floor muscles to a count of ten, hold them for a count of ten, then relax and rest for a count of ten. Repeat ten times.

Fast
Lift your pelvic floor quickly, hold for a count of one, then relax and rest for a count of one. Repeat ten times.

4 Try to do a series of both fast and slow exercises six times a day.

Exercising at home

★ Buy a yoga or pilates DVD that is aimed at new mothers, put your baby in his bouncy chair and let him watch.

★ Use an exercise bike or step machine while you are watching TV.

★ Look online for a set of stretches and lifts you can do with your baby. Some will show you safe ways of lifting him as part of the routine.

Exercising outside

★ Walking with your pram is one of the simplest forms of exercise and your baby can enjoy it too. Invest in a pair of good trainers and walk with good posture – don't lean forwards or backwards, keep your bottom tucked in and your eyes straight ahead.

★ Ask your health visitor, or look online for local mother and baby yoga classes. These have gentle stretches for you and your baby to do together, and are a great way of meeting new friends with babies.

★ Pram-pushing exercise classes in local parks are a great way of getting exercise and meeting new people. The instructor will have tailor-made exercises for new mothers, and your baby will enjoy watching you!

★ When your postnatal bleeding has stopped, you can start swimming or try an aqua-aerobics class. Many gyms and pools have a crèche facility.

★ If you can't find a pool or gym with a crèche, share babycare with a friend. Take it in turns to look after your friend's baby for an hour while she works out, then swap. Having a regular time to exercise – and involving a friend – can help you stick to it.

Enjoying motherhood

Becoming a parent affects you in ways that it is hard to imagine before the birth of your baby. The learning curve is steep, the hours are long and the range of emotions you feel may not be quite what you expected. Some new parents take it all in their stride, while others find it harder to get used to the changes to their lifestyle. Things that you may be finding hard include:

- **Responsibility** – you are now in charge of another person who depends on you for survival.
- **Lack of routine** – everything revolves around your new baby and you may find yourself skipping showers and forgetting lunch while you wait for life to slow down.
- **Lifestyle change** – suddenly you can't just pop to the shops or go out for the evening if you feel like it. Everything needs to be planned in advance.
- **Physical demands** – you may still be recovering from the birth, or from your pregnancy, and sleepless nights will be taking their toll. It's easy to underestimate how much physical work is involved with looking after a baby – until you have one.
- **Commitment** – even if you are feeling tired and sick, your baby still needs changing and feeding.
- **Too much information** – new mothers are often overwhelmed by the amount of decisions they have to make about looking after their new babies. In many cases, they are given conflicting advice from health visitors, friends, family and their partners.

To help you cope with all the emotions you are feeling – both good and bad – it's a good idea to let them out. Talk to your partner or a friend or start writing a diary where you can express exactly how you are feeling. To be in control, you need to have confidence in yourself. This doesn't mean that you shouldn't ask for advice or help. It means being kind to yourself, and telling yourself regularly that you are a great mother, and that you are doing the best job you possibly can. Remember that everyone has times when they feel as if they are struggling to cope, but these moments pass. You are in the process of building an amazing bond with your baby, which is an exhilarating, if sometimes daunting, thing. Be proud!

Ideas to keep life fun

⭐ Keep taking photos. You can never have too many, and you can look forward to making a beautiful album to share with your baby – one day!

⭐ For an instant mood lifter, put on your favourite music and dance in the sitting room. Your baby will be happy to watch you.

⭐ Get a take-away and treat yourself to a picnic in the park with your baby. She will enjoy being out in the open and you will appreciate the change of scenery.

⭐ Phone your parents for a chat and talk about what you were like as a baby. Tell them all the things you enjoyed most and share some memories.

⭐ Once a while, indulge in some shopping. If you can't bear to go to the shops look online for things that will make you feel happy and relaxed.

⭐ Look out for baby screenings at your local cinema. These are usually in the morning and are for parents and young babies only and are an excellent chance to keep on top of the latest releases.

Note: Symptoms of postnatal depression include lethargy, insomnia, feelings of panic, detachment and an inability to cope. If you think that you may be depressed talk to your doctor or health visitor sooner rather than later as they will be able to help you. There is no point in struggling alone.

6
Months+

Your baby's development

At six months, your baby is halfway through his first year. He's eating solid foods and wanting to get mobile, so you'll need to start childproofing your house, and keep an eagle eye on the things he is putting in his mouth. This is the stage where he'll want to explore everything he comes across and by eleven months, your baby will be getting ready to walk.

> By eight months, your baby is starting to realise that he has his own personal likes and dislikes – so he may scowl when you offer him a certain food, then smile when you switch to another!

Six months

Your baby will want to get moving and may be able to roll, or push himself up on his hands and knees. This is the age that teething often begins, so your baby might be very dribbly or start waking in the night if he was previously sleeping through.

Seven months

Your baby will be able to use his hands to clap, scoop up a toy or hold a cup and drink from it. He may love to bounce and could be sitting unassisted. He may get 'stranger anxiety' – suddenly becoming unhappy about meeting new people, or getting upset when he is left with someone other than you. This will pass in a few months.

Eight months

Your baby may be starting to crawl – or shuffle on his bottom, or wriggle on his tummy – to get around. He will be able to pick up small objects, so keep small objects that he might choke on out of his reach.

Nine months

Your baby may be pulling himself up to standing and cruising around the furniture. He can hand objects to you and will enjoy playing with building bricks that can be stacked up and knocked down.

Ten months

Your baby's babbling will start to sound more like real words, and he will love trying to have a conversation with you. He may be getting more adventurous and interested in climbing, particularly up the stairs and maybe over the rail of his cot. He could start to protest about things that he was fine with before – like being put in his pushchair!

Eleven months

Your baby may be able to walk if you hold on to his hand, and will be enjoying his new sense of independence. He will understand the word 'no' – but he may not stop what he is doing when he hears it! Try to use it sparingly. He may even be able to say 'no' back to you by now – it is a common first word among babies.

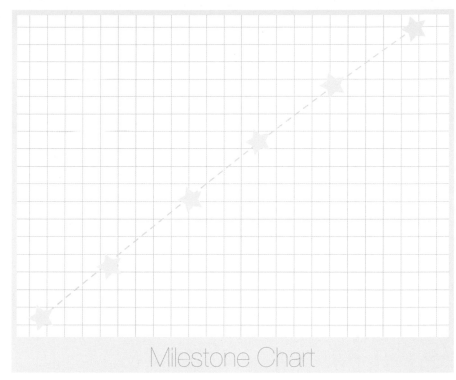

Your baby
learns to walk

Your baby learns to
drop things

Your baby will
respond to your
voice from across
the room

Your baby will start
teething, crawling
and pulling
himself upright

Your baby will sit
without support

Your baby will start
to eat solid food

Milestone Chart

6 months   6-8 months   6-9 months   7 months   9-11 months   10-18 months

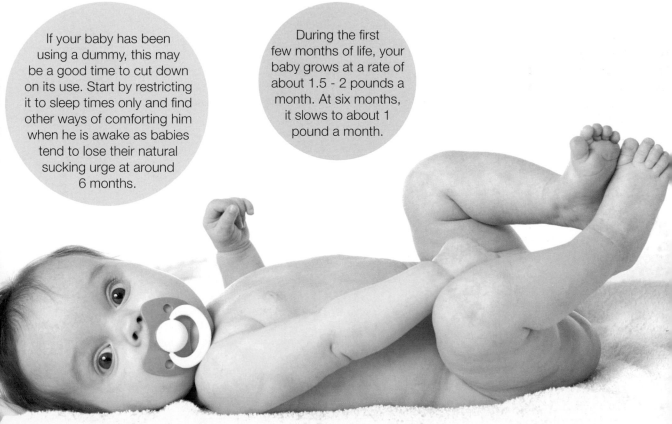

If your baby has been
using a dummy, this may
be a good time to cut down
on its use. Start by restricting
it to sleep times only and find
other ways of comforting him
when he is awake as babies
tend to lose their natural
sucking urge at around
6 months.

During the first
few months of life, your
baby grows at a rate of
about 1.5 - 2 pounds a
month. At six months,
it slows to about 1
pound a month.

Weaning your baby

As she eat more solids, your baby will want less milk, but you should continue to breastfeed or give 500-600ml (a pint) of formula a day until she is twelve months old. This usually works out as one bottle or feed in the morning and one before she goes to bed. Teach your baby to drink from a cup and make sure that she drinks water, or well-diluted juice at regular intervals throughout the day. An open cup or a sippy cup with no valve is better for her teeth.

Helping your baby

Your child gets more than just food out of breastfeeding. She gets to spend special time with her mother that is comforting and reassuring, and this may be a reason why she doesn't want it to stop. Try spending time with your baby in other ways that she will find reassuring. Playing games, singing and cuddling together or reading a book will show her that she can still spend one-on-one time with you, and is not going to lose out on the closeness. If your child is sick or feeling unsettled – for example if you have gone back to work, she has started nursery or you have moved house – you may want to consider breastfeeding for a while longer, and wait for things to settle down. Major life events can make weaning more difficult, but if you try again in a few weeks and you may get better results.

Cutting down on breastfeeding

If you have enjoyed the close bond that breastfeeding brings you might find stopping an emotional experience. Part of you may be glad that you are getting your body back, another part very sad that it's all over. Some mothers choose to continue breastfeeding for a long time after their child has started eating solids, allowing their child to decide when they want to stop.

In some cases, it only takes a few weeks to stop breastfeeding, as your baby may be ready for the change. In other cases, your baby might find the transition hard and it can take longer. You should aim to cut down on feeds gradually, rather than just suddenly stopping. This could be distressing for your baby and painful for you, as your breasts may become engorged and there is a danger of mastitis.

When you first start weaning, you will be offering your baby solids after you've breastfed her. As soon as she is eating well, you can switch this round and offer her milk after her meal. Eventually, you can replace the breastfeed with a drink of water. You will still be feeding your baby in the morning and before bed, but try to resist the temptation to 'comfort feed' her at snack times, when she could be eating solid food instead.

Note: If you want to stop breastfeeding before your baby is one, you'll need to give her formula milk.

First foods

Today, most experts agree that you shouldn't introduce solids for the first six months of your baby's life. Breastmilk or formula will meet all their nutritional needs and the risk of allergies may increase if food is introduced too soon. Very young babies can't control their tongue or throat muscles and may choke on food, but at six months your baby will be giving you signals that he is ready for solids, such as eyeing up the food on your plate!

Note: With all weaning, you should continue with milk feeds to meet your baby's nutritional needs and only decrease when she starts to eat more.

Start with first foods such as:

* Cereals – baby rice mixed with milk.
* Mashed cooked vegetables – potato, yam, sweet potato, carrot.
* Mashed fruit – banana, avocado, cooked apple or pear.

Once your baby is used to eating these, you should add other foods, such as:

* Mashed meat, fish and chicken.
* Mashed rice, noodles and pasta.
* Lentils (dhal).
* Full-fat dairy products – yoghurt, fromage frais and custard.

By nine months, your baby should be able to eat 'adult' food such as sandwiches, pasta shapes, fish fingers, risotto etc.

Note: Prepare large quantities in advance and freeze them in ice cube trays to save time. Then you can defrost and heat them as you need. It is not safe to reheat or refreeze leftovers.

Do NOT feed your baby:

* Salt – this is bad for their kidneys.
* Sugar – this can lead to tooth decay.
* Honey – avoid honey until your baby is 12 months old.
* Nuts – whole nuts, including peanuts, can choke your baby.
* Low fat foods – your baby needs the calories in full fat milk, cheese and yoghurt.
* Saturated fat – this is found in crisps, chips, cakes etc.
* Shark, swordfish and marlin – these contain too much mercury for your baby.
* Raw shellfish – this can increase the risk of food poisoning.
* Eggs – your baby can eat cooked eggs from six months, if solid, not runny.

Step by Step

1 Make sure your baby is sitting up and facing forward, preferably in a highchair.

2 Start by offering a few baby spoons of food, once a day, after a milk feed.

3 Mix a small amount of baby rice with his usual milk, testing to ensure it is not too hot.

4 Do not force your baby. Wait for him to open his mouth when the food is offered. If he doesn't seem to want to eat, just wait and try again later.

5 Try different foods at each meal to add variety. Do not worry if your baby seems to dislike certain foods. Just leave it and try them again in a few days.

6 Allow a couple of weeks for your baby to get used to the idea, then move on to offering solid food two and then three times a day. Aim for three meals a day by seven months.

7 Let your baby use his fingers to feed himself as soon as he shows an interest. It is good for him to explore the different textures and get a bit messy!

Baby-lead weaning

This means letting your baby feed himself instead of feeding him purées and mashed up food. Instead, offer him a wide range of finger foods to try such as chunks of banana, avocado, carrots and pumpkin. At first, your baby may just play with the food – it can be messy and a lot of the food might end up on the floor, but he will enjoy experiencing all the different tastes and textures.

Visiting the dentist

You should take your baby to visit the dentist by her first birthday, or within six months of her first tooth appearing. It is unlikely that she will need treatment but you can make sure that everything is developing the right way. It's a good idea to get your child used to the dentist from an early age. If you are nervous about going, your child is likely to pick up on this, so try not to show that you are scared.

At your visit, the dentist will examine your child's gums and jaw, look at any existing teeth for decay, and check her bite. If she is nervous, you can sit in the chair and hold her in your lap. Many dentists will want to see your child every six months, to monitor the development of her teeth, and to build up her confidence with each visit.
You should brush your baby's teeth as soon as they come through. You will need a baby toothbrush and fluoride toothpaste – you can get fruit or mint flavours. Don't worry if you don't manage much brushing at the start. It's more important that your baby sees brushing as part of her daily routine.

Preventing tooth decay

★ Tooth decay is caused by sugar in sweet food and drinks. Sweets and lollipops are especially harmful because your baby's teeth are frequently in contact with the sugar while she sucks them.

★ From the time your baby is weaned, she should be encouraged to eat savoury snacks. Remember that there is often sugar in savoury pre-packaged baby foods and drinks.

★ Try not to offer your baby sweets or biscuits as treats. Bubbles and stickers make good alternatives.

★ If children are having sweets or chocolate, it's less harmful for their teeth if they eat the sweets all at once and at the end of a meal rather than eating them little by little and/or between meals.

★ Avoid drinks that contain artificial sweeteners such as saccharin or aspartame, or make sure that they are very well diluted.

★ A beaker with a free-flow lid is a better choice than a beaker with a teat or a non-spill valve. This will help your child to sip instead of suck, which is better for her teeth. A bottle should only be used for milk or water.

Note: Sucking on bottles that contain sweetened drinks is one of the biggest causes of tooth decay in young children.

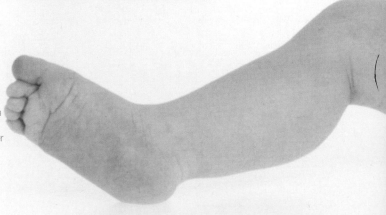

Check the label on food and drink that you give to your baby. If it contains sugar, it may be written in a number of ways, such as sucrose, glucose, dextrose, maltose, fructose, hydrolysed starch, invert sugar, honey, raw sugar, brown sugar, cane sugar, muscovado and concentrated fruit juices. Maltodextrin is not a sugar but can cause tooth decay.

Step by Step

1 Babies only need a tiny smear of toothpaste and children a pea-sized amount.

2 Hold your baby on your knee with her head on your chest.

3 Brush her teeth in small circles covering all the surfaces.

4 Let your child spit the toothpaste out afterwards. Rinsing with water can reduce the benefits of fluoride.

5 Brush your baby's teeth twice a day, in the morning and before bed.

6 You should help your child brush her teeth until she is around seven years old.

Moving out of your bedroom

Experts advise that your baby should sleep in a cot in the same room as you for the first six months of his life. However, when you decide the time is right to move your baby, it's not realistic to expect him to sleep as easily on his own as he did in your room. Try to be patient as your baby gets used to his new room. Any change in routine can affect your baby's sleeping, and this is a big change!

Try not to let your baby back into your bed if you have decided the time has come to stop co-sleeping. It will make him think that he can get what he wants by crying which will not help you stick to your plan. Be consistent!

1. If your baby has been sleeping in your bed, or a crib, move him into his cot, but keep it next to your bed where he can still see you.

2. When you feel ready, move the cot into his room, but sleep next to him on a mattress or camp bed for a few nights.

3. Sleep in separate rooms.

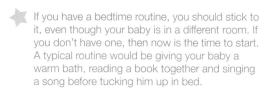

If you have a bedtime routine, you should stick to it, even though your baby is in a different room. If you don't have one, then now is the time to start. A typical routine would be giving your baby a warm bath, reading a book together and singing a song before tucking him up in bed.

If your baby cries as soon as you leave the room, try a more gradual approach to leaving. Put your baby down in her cot, then stay in the room while he gets comfy. Sit on a chair next to the bed quietly, letting your presence reassure him as he drops off. The next night, move the chair closer to the door, then the night after a little further away, until you are out of the room completely.

Try to be realistic. If your baby is sick, he may need to come back into your room for a while. Don't let this worry you, you can pick up from where you left off or try again when he is better.

Give your baby a blanket or teddy that he can snuggle up to. Try sleeping with it in your bed for a couple of nights beforehand so that it has your scent. Your baby will find this comforting.

91

Baby sign language

Baby sign language is a way of teaching your baby how to communicate using simple hand movements. Gestures are a normal part of communication and most babies pick them up, and will happily wave 'bye bye' to a friend or hold up their arms when they want to be lifted up.

With baby sign language, your baby will be able to understand and perform simple gestures before she learns to speak, which has benefits for her and for you. Being able to tell you that she is hungry, tired or thirsty will help her feel less frustrated and fussy.

Don't worry that teaching your baby to sign will slow down her speech development. Studies have shown that signing may help your baby learn to talk and add a lot more words to her vocabulary.

Where to learn?

There may be a baby signing class nearby that you can attend, which usually involves singing, hand puppets, and a chance to socialise with other parents afterwards. Otherwise, you can look for an online course or buy a book. There are several different systems to choose from, but it shouldn't matter which you pick as long as you stick to it. Often, your baby will start to approximate signs that you have learned so that he has his own special way of doing them. This is fine – as long as you understand what she means, you are communicating, and that's the goal!

Simple sentence

Try telling your baby that you love her, using sign language. Say 'I' – point to your chest, 'love' – cross your hands over your chest, 'you' – point to your baby.

Here are some simple signs you could try with your baby, based on ASL (American sign language):

Love
Cross your arms over your chest in an X shape.

Biscuit
Hold out your left palm side up. Ima this is some doug Use your right ha act out using a c cutter to cut a sha from the dough – it down, lift, rotate bring it down aga

Step by Step

1 Start with a sign that refers to something your baby will want – such as milk.

2 Make the milk sign before you feed your baby, saying the world out loud as you make the sound. Keep your expression animated and your voice enthusiastic.

3 Feed your baby her milk straight away. If he has a break during feeding, make the milk sign and say the word again before she starts again.

4 When your baby has finished feeding, say the word and make the sign one last time.

5 When you see your baby making the sign for milk, you should give her lots of praise and encouragement, and feed her straight away.

Ball
Bring your hands together with your fingers touching to make a ball shape.

Milk
Form a C shape with your hand and squeeze it into a fist, two times – as if you were milking a cow.

Learning to walk

Some babies take their first few steps as young as 9 months, others as late as 18 months, but most babies find their feet around the time of their first birthday. Learning to walk is an important step towards independence for your baby and a sign that he is leaving babyhood behind and becoming a toddler. There are several stages that he will go through as he learns:

- Your baby starts trying to pull himself up while holding tightly on to furniture.
- He works out how to cruise around the room, holding on to the edge of sofas, chairs and coffee tables to keep his balance.
- He learns to let go and stand still, but may not be able to move or sit down by himself!
- He takes his first few steps.
- He learns how to stoop down and pick up a toy, then stand up again.

It's usual for some babies to go back to crawling for a short while after they have taken their first steps. Walking is a new skill that takes a lot of concentration and practice. Let your baby move at his own speed, giving him lots of praise and encouragement to build his confidence. If you're concerned about your child's late walking, and he is over 19 months old, you could ask your doctor for a medical examination which will look at his development in the context of other skills.

Baby walkers

Safety experts discourage the use of baby walkers, because of the number of accidents and injuries they cause. Most problems are caused when the baby walker tips, and the baby is thrown downstairs, or crashes into furniture, heaters or ovens. Using a walker won't help your baby learn to walk and he will learn better if allowed to exercise and play safely on the floor.

Helping your baby

★ When your baby can stand, let him try walking in front of you while you hold his hands for support. You can take away one hand every now and then to let her practise her balance.

★ If your baby is standing on his own, give him lots of smiles and encouragement to see if he will try walking towards you. Don't be upset if he just sits down on his bottom, treat it as a fun game that you are playing together.

★ When your baby has learned to cruise you can arrange furniture in a way that will help him to practise crossing the room. Make sure you pick sturdy items that won't fall over!

★ Your baby might get stuck standing up and cry for help. Don't just bump him down, show him how to bend his knees and sit. It may take a bit of practice but he'll get the hang of it.

★ You can encourage your baby to walk by standing or kneeling in front of him and helping him walk towards you, holding your hands.

★ Try to keep the floor clear so that there is room for your baby to practise walking. Check for hazards that might cause him to trip or injure himself.

★ Find a push-along toy, such as a brick truck, for your baby to hold on to and push. Make sure that it is stable and will not easily fall over.

★ Let your baby spend time barefoot, as this will help him to improve his sense of balance.

★ When you buy shoes for your baby, find a shop with a qualified fitter who will measure his feet. There should be room for growth in the shoe, and it should be supportive and comfortable. Tight socks and shoes can stop your baby's feet growing properly.

Note: Childproof your home so that it is safe for your baby to walk around. Put stair gates at the top and bottom of the stairs.

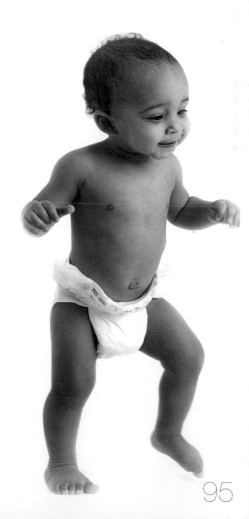

Having fun with your baby

Your growing baby is getting more interested in toys but she is still most happy when playing with you. She can now see a full range of colours, although brightly-coloured toys may still be the most appealing to her, and the chances are that she will be putting everything she is interested in into her mouth!

Six months

Make simple finger puppets by cutting the fingers off an old pair of gloves and gluing on eyes, ears and a mouth. Give them silly names and funny voices, and make them talk, kiss, tickle and dance on your baby. Pretend to have a conversation with them, switching between your real voice and your puppet-voice as you talk.

Seven months

Your baby will love exploring and emptying out bags. Fill an empty bag with interesting objects, such as jam jar lids, plastic bottles and containers – use anything that you find around the house that is safe, and try to get a variety of textures, sizes and shapes. Now let your baby empty the bag and play with the contents.

Note: Plastic bags are a suffocation risk – never leave your baby playing with one.

Eight months

Action songs are a great way to have fun with your baby. Try nursery rhymes such as 'Round and Round the Garden' or 'Hickory Dickory Dock'. Use your hand to act them out, running your fingers up your baby's arm when you sing that the mouse ran up the clock. Try old favourites like 'This Little Piggy' where you count your baby's toes, then tickle her at the end.

Nine months

Have fun together with a small teddy or toy. Practise turn-taking as you hand your baby a toy and see if she hands it back again. Hand it to her upside

down and encourage her to turn it the right way up. Let her watch you hide the toy in a box or under a blanket then let her try to find it.

Ten months

Collect old cereal boxes, bowls, yoghurt pots and other household scrap – you can paint them bright colours if you are feeling creative! Use them to build a tower together. Be as creative as you can, but don't get too attached to it – your baby will love knocking it all down when you've finished!

Eleven months

On a sunny day, take your baby outside with a jug of water and some large paintbrushes and show her how to paint with water. You can paint a bench, wall, stool or even just the floor. Join in and draw simple circles and shapes to encourage her.

Going abroad with your baby

You probably won't want to do much travelling with your baby at first, but there are a lot of good reasons for taking a holiday while your baby is still young. He is portable, easy to feed and will be happy to be pushed around in his pram or carried in a sling for most of the day – you don't need to get into the world of child-friendly hotels and kids clubs just yet. If you are going somewhere sunny, don't forget to pack your baby's sun cream and sunhat. You are likely to have a lot more luggage than you are used to, so try to keep clothes to a minimum and pack a tube of travel wash.

What to pack:

- A smaller bag with nappy, wipes and nappy sacks to take to the toilet.
- A new toy or baby book that will keep your baby amused.
- Your baby's favourite blanket or toy.
- Enough milk or food for the whole trip.

You might be lucky and find that your baby falls asleep on the plane. Try to feed your baby during take off and landing as the swallowing motion will help with any ear popping. A dummy will help with this as well. If your baby won't sleep, walk up and down the plane to give her a chance to look around, or calm down if she seems upset. Don't let your baby get bored. Games to play in the seat like peek-a-book or action songs will work wonders, and you don't have to do them too loudly!

Your baby will need his own passport if you want to go abroad. It will be valid for five years, even if it has a baby photo of him on it! Remember that it takes about four weeks for your passport to come through, so don't leave it until the last minute.

You will need:
- An application form from the post office, or online.
- Two identical colour photos of your baby. One must be signed on the back by a professional (such as a teacher, lawyer, accountant, doctor etc) who owns a current UK passport and who knows you and your baby.
- Documents to prove your baby is British, such as his birth certificate.
- Passport details for you and your partner.
- Payment.

The photo needs to show your baby's face against a plain white background with no toys or dummies or other people in the picture. Try lying him down on a white sheet to take the picture or, your local high-street photographer or pharmacy will be able to do it for you.

Plane travel tips

★ There is no standard minimum age for babies to fly. Many airlines will take a baby from two weeks old, or some even younger, but it's best to check their requirements if your baby is very young as you may need a doctor's note:

★ Don't forget that you will need a few weeks to organise a passport for your baby if you want to leave the country.

★ Your baby will need his own ticket, even if he does not have his own seat. Some airlines may take a baby for no extra charge, but others will charge a percentage of an adult ticket.

★ You will need to ask about baggage allowances – otherwise you may have to pay extra if your baby is not allowed a bag of his own.

★ Ask for a bulkhead seat if possible, as this is the row that has no seats in front of it. Some airlines have carrycots for babies to sleep in, usually on long haul flights. You should request one when you book your ticket.

★ If your baby has his own seat booked, you can use a car seat on it for him to sleep in, but check with the airline first.

★ Most aeroplanes have changing tables in the toilets, which may be cramped, but better than doing it at your seat.

★ Make sure that you pack a lot of nappies and a few changes of spare clothes, including a spare set for you in case of accidents.

★ Baby food will be available on the plane, but you might want to bring your own baby spoon.

★ If you are formula feeding, take the powder rather than ready-mixed cartons and make it up on board. The crew will warm bottles or boil water for you.

★ Check with your airline about liquid restrictions. You should be able to bring expressed breastmilk, formula or cow's milk or boiled water in a baby bottle on board. But you may be asked to taste it.

★ Hand baggage restrictions apply to baby items such as nappy cream, so only take a small container, under 100ml.

★ Pushchairs are not usually counted as part of your luggage. Your baby can stay in it till you get to the plane, then hand it in to the cabin crew. You can collect it again at the end of the flight.

Childproofing your house

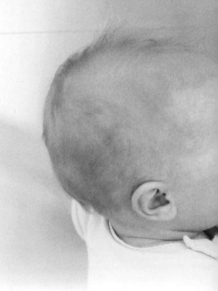

Your home is the place where most accidents are likely to happen. And as soon as your baby gets mobile, she can get into trouble. Supervision is the best way to prevent injuries, but even the most watchful parents can't watch their children every single second of the day.

The best way to work out what is dangerous in your house is to give yourself a baby's eye view of it all. Get down on your hands and knees and crawl around the house, trying to see it as a baby would. What can you reach? What looks tempting? What could you pick up and put in your mouth? Where could you put your finger? When you've worked out where the problem areas are, you can fix them and make your home a safer place for your baby – there are many childproofing kits available to buy.

Kitchen

- Keep sharp tools, such as knives, forks and scissors in a drawer with a childproof latch.
- Use a childproof latch on your washing machine, oven, fridge and dishwasher.
- Put knob protectors over the oven knobs.
- Keep cords and wires out of reach.
- Move any small fridge magnets that might be swallowed.
- Use a childproof latch on your bin, or the cupboard with your bin in.
- Keep the following things stored out of reach: glass items, appliances with blades, matches and lighters, vitamins and medicine, cleaning liquids and detergents, insect sprays, alcohol, plastic bags.
- Remember to keep the handle of the pan turned away from the room while you cook.

Bathroom

- Keep the following stored out of reach or in a drawer with a childproof lock: razor blades, nail scissors, sharp tools, medication, all bottles of toiletries, all bottles of bathroom cleaners, hairdryers and straighteners etc, electric razors
- Attach a childproof latch to the toilet seat and bin.
- Keep the toilet brush somewhere out of reach, as children often love to play with these.

Bedroom

- Keep all cords and wires tied up out of reach.
- Attach a lid support to the toy chest to stop it slamming shut.
- Make sure the night light is out of reach and isn't touching any fabric.
- Keep the following things stored out of reach: medication, coins, scissors, all small or sharp objects.

Staircase

* Attach safety gates to the top and bottom of the stairs.
* Keep stairs clear of tripping hazards.
* Make sure that your baby can't fit through banisters or railings.
* Make sure banisters and railings are secure.

General

* Install a finger pinch guard on doors.
* Make sure your baby cannot open the outside door by herself.
* Add childproof locks to sliding doors.
* Use safety bars or window guards on windows where necessary.
* Attach anti-slip pads to rugs.
* Secure bookshelves, wardrobes and other furniture to the wall so they can't be tipped.
* Stick protective padding to the corners of coffee tables or other furniture with sharp edges.

* Remove any poisonous houseplants – look online for a list.
* Buy a carbon monoxide detector.
* Install a working smoke alarm in each room.
* Check them regularly.
* Put a safety plug in all unused plug sockets.
* Cover radiators with childproof screens if necessary.
* Put a firescreen around a working fireplace.
* Put a list of emergency numbers near the phone.

Keeping up your relationship

Having a baby is bound to change your relationship with your partner. When you're feeling tired, stressed or busy, your personal life can seem to vanish overnight. But with a little thought and a few small changes you can make a big difference. Start by opening up your definition of romance to include the everyday gestures that you and your partner make – such as giving your partner time to have a relaxing bath, choosing a movie to watch together on television, or offering to cook, clean and empty the dishwasher. Here are some other ideas to help you keep romance alive.

Have a conversation

Try to have at least one chat a day about something that doesn't involve your baby. Your or your partner's work, what's in the news, music or books are all great. Baby stuff is off limits – for a while.

Keep touching

Touch goes a long way towards making each other feel loved and reassured. A quick hug when you wake up in the morning, a kiss before you go to sleep, rubbing each other's shoulders when you're watching television or holding hands when you're out are all simple ways of staying connected.

Make a date

If a friend or relative offers you a chance of babysitting, then take it. Go out for a walk, for a coffee, for a meal – whatever you can do in the time you have been given. If you have a friend who will look after your baby in the day, you could go to a matinee at the theatre or cinema.

Take a walk

If your baby has regular naps, put one aside for a romantic walk with your partner. While your baby sleeps in the buggy you can take time to stroll and chat like you used to. Stay away from busy shopping centres or noisy roads!

Set aside time

Put aside ten minutes each day to spend together. Sit together and really pay attention to what your partner is saying. Don't use this time to make 'to do' lists or remind each other about chores or to go through your diaries. Just try to connect.

Give each other a break

Take it in turns to let each other have time to themselves. You could take your baby for a walk while they have a nap, or stay in with your baby while they go to a coffee shop and read the paper for an hour. Let each other have an evening off to see friends, even if it's only for a short while.

Your sex life

Lack of privacy and lack of time are two big factors in the failure to restart your sex life after having a baby. For many parents, given the choice between getting some extra sleep or having sex, sleep wins every time. However, it's a good idea to keep up your sexual connection with your partner – after all, it's probably what brought you together in the first place.

Remember that sex doesn't have to be a long, drawn out affair. If you both fancy a quickie before you go to bed, then that's fine! You may have more time to have sex at the weekends, during your baby's daytime naps. Try to keep a sense of humour if your baby wakes up during sex – it's probably happened to most parents at one time or another.

12
Months+

Your baby's development

During these months your child goes from baby to toddler, and you will find your life evolving as you adapt to her changes. This is the time of tantrums, messy mealtimes and constant chasing after her, but it is also a very rewarding stage, as your child becomes more and more responsive, and her personality really starts to emerge.

Your child is likely to use both hands equally at the moment, so you will not know if she is right handed or left handed for some time yet.

Don't worry if your toddler looks bow legged when she walks. This is perfectly normal while she is growing and it can take a while for her legs to take on their permanent appearance.

Twelve months

Your baby will soon be walking, if she isn't up and about already. She can understand a lot of what you are saying and will be able to point to parts of her body when asked.

Thirteen months

A lot of your baby's games are about exploring the world, as she drops things on the floor to see you pick them up, or imitates your gestures – including hugs and kisses! Your baby may start to eat less as her growth slows down.

Fourteen months

At this stage, your baby is likely to enjoy pushing objects – such as chairs or boxes – around and is constantly testing her physical abilities. She will be testing boundaries too and you may find her becoming stubborn when it comes to putting on a hat or eating her meals!

Fifteen months

Your baby is learning that she is an individual and will enjoy recognising herself in a mirror. She can say quite a few words now – including 'no!' – and should enjoy imaginary play. If you hand her a spoon, she may pretend to eat with it, or if you give her a brush, she may brush a doll's hair.

Sixteen months

Your baby can walk, run, climb and understand basic rules. But don't worry if she is starting to have tantrums. The so-called 'terrible twos' often start earlier than two, and these outbursts will be normal for a while yet as your child copes with the frustrations of the world.

Seventeen months

Your baby is growing up! She may be dropping one of her daytime naps and learning how to dress herself. However, she is far from grown up, and may start going through a fussy eating stage or learning to scream!

Your baby will enjoy building stacks of bricks

Your baby will want to try feeding and dressing himself

Your child may start to say words and understand them

Your baby will start to say words like 'mama' and 'dada'

Milestone Chart

| 12 months | 12-18 months | 13-15 months | 15-18 months |

Get into the habit of strapping your toddler in to her high chair, even if she complains. As she becomes more mobile, she is likely to start experimenting with climbing out if your back is turned.

Feeding your toddler

Your child is growing up and he's ready to eat the same foods as the rest of the family – although he'll still need you to cut it up into smaller pieces for quite a while yet! It's important to set a good example to your child by including him in family meal times where you all eat the same food. If you make distinctions between children's food and adult's food, your child may feel that there are things he shouldn't eat. He should be happy to try a wide variety of food at the moment, so offer him whatever you are eating and see what he likes.

Sample meal plan for your toddler:

Breakfast:
Fruit
Iron-fortified baby cereal
Toast and butter with an egg
Whole milk

Morning snack:
Raisins
Cheese
Breadsticks

Lunch:
Minced beef (or other protein if your child is vegetarian)
Potato
Chopped vegetables
Fruit
Whole milk

Afternoon snack:
Toast and butter
Whole milk

Dinner:
Pasta with chicken (or other protein if your child is vegetarian)
Chopped vegetables
Yoghurt
Whole milk

Evening snack:
Whole milk

Plenty of starchy foods

Some dairy food and protein

A small amount of food high in fat and sugar

Plenty of fruit and vegetables

This is a guide to the proportions of food that make up a balanced diet.

A toddler's diet

Your child's stomach is a lot smaller than yours, which is why he needs three balanced meals a day, plus several healthy snacks to keep him going. He needs a diet that is high in fat and low in fibre, which is very filling. If he eats too much fibre, he may not get all the nutrients he needs from other foods.

Your child should have a third the amount of salt that is recommended for adults – 2g a day. Never add salt to baby food and remember not to add it to a family meal if your child is eating with you. Check the label before feeding your child prepared adult food, as it is often very high in salt. Look at the figure for salt (or sodium) per 100g. High salt levels are more than 1.5g salt per 100g (or 0.6g sodium) and low salt levels are 0.3g salt or less per 100g (or 0.1g sodium). Two digestive biscuits contain one fifth of your child's daily allowance of salt!

Note: Your child should still avoid artificial flavourings, colourings, preservatives and sweeteners, uncooked eggs, shellfish and whole nuts.

A balanced diet for a toddler is made up of these foods:
- Starchy foods – bread, rice, cereals and potatoes.

- Fruit and vegetables – try to offer a range of different colours and textures as they all contain different nutrients.

- Dairy foods – milk, cheese and yoghurt are rich in calcium which your child needs to grow strong. You should aim for three portions of dairy food a day.

- Protein – meat, fish, eggs and pulses. Your child should have two servings (three servings for vegetarians) a day.

Note: Biscuits and cakes are high in fat and sugar and low in vitamins and minerals, and should be eaten in moderation.

Coping with nighttime waking

Sleep is very important to your baby's wellbeing. A tired baby will be disagreeable, prone to mood swings or hyperactive – and the chances are you will be too. If your nighttime routine is not working for you, it is important to think carefully about what you are doing and see what changes you can make to help your baby meet his sleep needs in a way that works with your family set-up. Try to stay flexible – if what you are doing doesn't work, it's time to change. But remember that one approach will not work with all babies, or even with the same baby at different stages of his development.

In the early months, many babies sleep better when they are swaddled tightly in a blanket. But older babies often prefer looser clothes and coverings. If he gets too hot in the night, your baby will wake up.

If you feel that you really need extra help, you could consider hiring a night nanny who can provide short-term overnight support, or look online for a baby sleep consultant in your area. They will come to your house and advise you on establishing a routine that works for your baby. Costs will vary according to the region you live in.

Too much excitement and stimulation just before bedtime can wake your child up again, even if they were sleepy. Spend some time winding down and doing some calmer activities, like reading.

Check on the temperature and humidity of your baby's room. A relative humidity of around 50 percent is best and a warm-mist vaporiser in his room can help with this. Your baby may also find the white noise it makes soothing. A room that is slightly on the cooler side, at approximately 65 degrees Fahrenheit is more conducive to sleep.

If you are breastfeeding, and want to stop night feeds, ask your partner or a close friend who knows your baby well to help you out for a few nights and take over night duty. They won't be tempted to feed your baby, because they don't have the milk.

Try helping your baby to settle using touch. Pat her back or bottom gently and rhythmically to match your heartbeat. Then leave your hands on her back with a reassuring pressure. Gradually make the pressure lighter and lighter, then finally lift off, but stay sitting beside her for a short while before leaving the room.

Some toddlers are so busy playing during the day that they forget to eat, then wake up in the night because they are hungry. Feed your baby healthy snacks during the day, and offer him a bowl of porridge or cereal before bed to keep him topped up.

Approximate sleep requirements for your baby's age

Birth to three months

Your baby will sleep anything from 8 to 18 hours a day and wake to feed during the night.

Three to six months

Some babies will sleep for eight hours or longer at night.

Six to twelve months

Night feeds are no longer necessary and some babies will sleep for 12 hours at night as well as having two daytime naps.

Two years

Your baby may sleep 11 to 12 hours at night, with one or two naps in the daytime.

Three to four years

Your baby needs between 8 and 14 hours sleep. Some still nap during the day.

Talking to your baby

Between the age of 12 and 18 months, your baby's first single words will appear among the babbling noises, for example 'dad' or 'dog'. It may sound like he is speaking in another language, but it is important to listen to him and encourage his attempts to communicate. On average, a baby will be able to say between 10 and 20 words by the time he is 18 months old. Studies have shown that at this age, children can even pick out sentences that are grammatically correct, despite only being able to speak in one or two-word sentences themselves.

Your baby is learning that his gestures can help himself be understood, so he will start to shake his head for no, wave goodbye or hello, and point at an object that he wants.

This is the stage when your baby will surprise you by his ability to respond to questions and commands. Although he can't answer you yet, he will be happy to oblige if you ask him something simple such as: 'Kick the ball' or 'Bring me the cup'. Try playing a pointing game with your baby, asking him to touch parts of his body in turn – such as nose, eyes, ears – and watch him respond.

The more that you talk to your baby, the faster his vocabulary will grow as he starts to make connections between objects in the world and the names you give them. Try these ways to keep talking:

* Count the steps of the stairs as you climb them.
* Name fruit and vegetables in the supermarket while you shop.
* Say the colours of parked cars together as you walk down the street.
* Read a picture book together and see if your baby can point to the objects as you name them.
* Walk in the park and name all the animals you can see together – squirrel, pigeon, cat, dog.
* Offer simple choices, such as asking your baby if he wants to wear his red socks or his blue socks.
* Play a game where you pretend to talk to each other on the telephone.
* Build a tower of bricks, counting the blocks and naming the colours.
* Make some simple flash cards to play with, using common words such as milk, hat and boots.
* Repetition is a useful part of learning, so action rhymes and songs are a great way to have fun and learn together.

Most common first words:

- Dada
- Mama
- Hello
- Doggy
- Ball
- No
- Bye-bye
- Duck
- Uh-oh
- Car

The 'd' sound is easier for a baby to make, which explains why 'dada' – and sometimes 'duck' and 'dog' often come before 'mama'.

Reading books

It's never too early to introduce your baby to books. When you spend time reading to your baby, you are teaching her about communication; introducing concepts such as colours, letter, shapes and numbers; helping her listening skills, concentration and vocabulary; and giving her information about the world. You are also giving her the thing that she enjoys most of all – one-to-one time together.

By 12 months, your baby may show an interest in turning the pages of the book herself. She will start to point at pictures and repeat sounds. If you have been reading to her often, she will have a favourite book by now, and love hearing it over and over again. Make sure there are books in your baby's toy box for her to pull out when she wants to. Babies like books with rhymes, or simple repetitive text. You can buy board books, cloth books, books that squeak and rattle, or books to take in the bath.

Don't forget to recite traditional nursery rhymes to your baby too. If you think you've forgotten the words, look up these popular songs online, or read these first lines and wait for the memories to come flooding back!

- Little Miss Muffet sat on a tuffet…
- Incey Wincey Spider climbed up the water spout…
- Baa Baa Black Sheep have you any wool?…
- Jack and Jill went up the hill to fetch a pail of water…
- The Grand Old Duke of York, he had ten thousand men…
- Humpty Dumpty sat on a wall…

By the time your baby is 12 months old, she has learned all the sounds she needs to be able to speak your language. The more words and stories you read, the better she will be able to talk when the time comes.

Reading tips

⭐ Make sure that you sit with your baby on your lap, or are cuddling her when you read so that she knows this is your special time together.

⭐ Don't be embarrassed to use an expressive voice – your baby will love it when you over-exaggerate words for effect, or use funny voices for different characters.

⭐ Ask your child questions about the book as you read. For example, 'Can you see the cat? What is he doing?' Don't worry if your child can't answer, provide the answers yourself and carry on reading: 'He's under the chair, isn't he!' By involving your child in the story you are laying the groundwork for future interactions.

⭐ Try to always read a story together before your baby's bedtime or naptime. It's also a great idea to have a book on hand if you are going to be going on a bus journey, spending time in a waiting room or in a long queue at the supermarket.

⭐ When reading to a young baby, you don't have to read the whole book. It's better to talk with your baby about the pictures or story and make it more of a conversation. Make sure that your baby can see your face as well as the pictures in the book.

⭐ At this age, don't be annoyed if your baby wants to start in the middle of a story, or change books half way through. Take her lead – the most important thing is that she is enjoying the books.

Playing together

Your baby can remember more, focus for longer and his arms and legs are constantly on the go! When your baby can walk, take him out to the park and let him get as much exercise as he can. Toys that can be pushed or pulled along are great for this age group, such as brick trucks or wheeled dogs on a lead.

Twelve months

Sort out one of your kitchen cupboards so that it only has baby-proof items in it – saucepans, pots, pan-lids and spoons are all great toys for your baby. He will love exploring the items in the cupboard, banging them into each other and putting them inside each other and back in the cupboard again.

Thirteen months

Play a simple game of hide-and-seek with your baby. You could hide one of his toys and help him find it, or hide yourself under a blanket or behind a door. Let your baby hide and pretend that you can't see him – his hiding place is likely to be obvious, and the same one again and again, but don't let him know that, and he will be delighted!

Fourteen months

Find an old handbag, and fill it with the sort of everyday handbag items your child is not usually allowed to touch. For example, keys that you don't mind losing, old credit cards or loyalty cards, a pad of sticky notes, empty lipstick tubes or powder compacts. (Make sure there is nothing your child can choke on.) Allow him to explore the bag, telling him what each item is and what it's used for, as he pulls it out.

Fifteen months

It's easy to make play-dough at home, by mixing together half a cup of salt, half a cup of water and one cup of flour. It won't harm your baby if it gets into his mouth by mistake. Play with the dough together – your baby will love squishing it in his hands. Make simple animal shapes using rolled out sausage shapes and balls and encourage your baby to make animal noises with you.

Sixteen months

Put down a large mat or sheets of newspaper and let your baby play with dry rice and lentils. Give him lots of different containers to use for pouring, scooping and filling. For example, plastic bowls and jars, measuring spoons, sieves and colanders and cake tins.

Seventeen months

Protect your table and floor with newspaper and let your child do handprints. Pour non-toxic paint into a plate and let him press his hand into it. Then help him to press his hand down on a large sheet of paper. He will be thrilled at the prints he is making and, when the paint is dry, you can get creative and add eyes, ears and tails to turn the prints into funny animals.

Travelling by car

Travelling with a young baby can be a challenge, but it's not impossible if you plan ahead. For a long journey by car, it's a good idea to travel at night, so that your baby can sleep as much as possible. If you are travelling in the day, try to plan the trip around nap times and meal times. If your child can sleep for most of the journey, that's a great help, but don't be tempted to let her sleep through your lunch stop – on a long trip, stopping to eat is just as good a break for your child as it is for you.

Note: Make sure that your baby's car seat is correct for size and age and is comfortable and safe. Never put a baby's seat in the front seat where the passenger air-bag is located.

Keep an eye on the temperature in the car, and dress your baby in layers so that it is easy to adjust his clothing accordingly.

Activate the child locks so that there is no chance your baby can work out how to open the doors.

Listen to music your baby will enjoy, or sing his favourite songs as you drive. Change the station on the radio if he gets upset.

Snacks, such as rice cakes and bread sticks will keep your baby occupied, but make sure that there is an adult sitting in the back with him while he eats, in case of choking.

Avoid rush hour and congested roads. Your baby will be much happier when the car is moving.

If you can, have another adult sit in the back with your baby, to reassure and entertain – and pick up the things that get thrown on the floor.

Sheets of colourful stickers are one of the best, mess-free ways of keeping your baby entertained on a long journey.

Take plenty of breaks. Let your baby out of the car to get a change of scenery and some exercise.

Always carry a first aid kit in your car.

If you find yourself becoming stressed, and your baby is crying and won't settle, pull over as soon as you can and take a break, to avoid causing an accident.

Before leaving, make sure that you have a bag with all the things your child might need within reach – not in the boot of the car.

You will need:

- Portable changing bag with nappies, wipes and disposal bags.
- Potty if your baby is toilet-trained.
- Pillows – to keep your baby comfortable.
- Plastic bucket – in case of travel sickness.
- Non-spill sippy bottle of water.
- Non-messy snacks.
- Blanket – to put on the ground for your baby to sit on if you have to stop.
- Your baby's favourite toy or blanket and a couple of new toys.
- Change of clothes for your baby – in case of accidents.
- Music your baby enjoys – nursery rhymes and songs.
- Bibs, baby bowls and spoons – in case you stop to eat in a café that doesn't cater for children.
- Your baby's regular milk in a cool-bag.

You may want to buy:

- Stick-on sunshades for your baby's window.
- A mirror that attaches to the headrest of the back seat, so you can see your baby from the front.
- Travel tray – this fits over your baby's car seat giving her an area to use for snacks, toys or colouring.
- Portable DVD player or tablet computer if your baby is old enough to enjoy cartoons.
- Portable highchair – this is a harness that attaches to an adult chair and turns it into a highchair. As it is made of cloth, it is very light and packs down small.
- If you are staying somewhere overnight, you may want to invest in travel black-out blinds for the windows.

Your baby's first birthday

Your baby's first birthday is a special one, and you are bound to want to celebrate. You can invite close friends and relatives, or friends with babies, but don't go overboard on numbers. Remember that your baby is still closely attached to you, and having too many people he doesn't know in his house could leave him feeling overwhelmed.

A good time for a party is the afternoon, after your baby's naptime. If he is tired, the party will be stressful for everyone – especially you! Try to keep everything – especially the food – as simple as possible. You should enjoy the party, and you won't be able to relax if you're stuck in the kitchen.

Party hints and tips

- Put away any breakable ornaments before the party.

- Keep watching out for hazards such as sharp forks, adults' hot or alcoholic drinks, or objects that could choke a baby and clear them away.

- Ask your friends to take photos, as you are likely to be too busy.

- Let breastfeeding friends know that they can feed their babies in your bedroom or another room if they want privacy.

- Set up a well-stocked nappy changing area in the bathroom or another room in the house.

- Keep lots of baby wipes on hand.

- Steer clear of party poppers and balloons – which are likely to pop and scare your younger guests.

- Limit the time of the party to 1-2 hours. More than this is too much for young babies to cope with.

If your house is too small for a party, you could hire a local community centre, church hall or sports club. If your child's birthday is in the summer, take picnic rugs to the local park and put bunting up in the trees and have your party there.

Invitations:

Get your baby involved in making the invitations. Cut out card shapes from plain coloured card, then let him scribble on them with his crayons, while you write out the party details on a smaller piece of paper. Glue the details on top of his drawings for a great, personalised invite.

Food:

Make a selection of finger foods that can be enjoyed by babies and adults. Keep the pieces small to avoid choking hazards – and don't put out bowls of peanuts. Try breadsticks and dips, mini sandwiches, and cubes of cheese and fruit and steer clear of too much sweet stuff. It's great if you want to make a cake, but don't feel embarrassed about buying one. Remember this is a celebration, not a competition. When you bring out the cake, keep the candle away from your baby, as he won't be able to blow it out and may try to grab at it.

Party bags:

You probably don't need to make up party bags for your guests at this age, but if you want to, remember that sweets and small toys are inappropriate for this age group. Instead you can give out stickers, crayons, bottles of bubble mixture or board books.

Activities and games:

Your baby is too young to really appreciate the classic party games like 'Pass the Parcel' or 'Musical Statues'. Set out toys in piles around the room for your younger guests to play with when they arrive. You could always put on music and have a dancing competition to get them moving later in the party.

Going back to work

Returning to work after maternity leave can be an emotional experience. You may be looking forward to spending some time being 'yourself' again, or you may feel unhappy about leaving your baby – and stressed when you think about the realities of being a working parent. However you are feeling, it's a good idea to plan ahead. So, before you go back:

- Try on your work outfits to see if they fit. If they don't, buy some new basics.
- Give yourself a couple of childcare days before you start work. This will also give you time to deal with any emotional responses you may have to leaving your baby.
- Ask your employer to phone or email you an update about what is going on at work so that you feel on top of things when you get back in.

Day-to-day tips

- Always work out what you and your baby are going to wear the night before.
- Do all your housework and ironing at weekends, and think about creating a schedule for you and your partner to share the housework. If you feel that your partner is not helping, talk to him about it politely. Sighing and rolling your eyes is not the same as explaining what is wrong, and your partner is unlikely to take the hint – which will leave you feeling angry and the work still not done! If you are finding the housework a big problem, consider getting a cleaner.
- Make to-do lists for everything – work and home.
- Use the internet for grocery shopping.
- Plan your week's meals in advance.
- Don't talk about work all the time at home and don't talk about your kids all the time at work.
- Try to get as many early nights as possible, and catch up on sleep at the weekend. You and your partner could take it in turns to have a lie-in, one on each day.

Work and your baby

★ Make sure you book your childcare well in advance. Many nurseries or childminders have long waiting lists and you want to be sure that your baby is being cared for in a place you are happy with – not the only place left with spaces.

★ Find out in advance what your employer's attitude is to you taking time off if your child is sick. They may allow compassionate leave, or you may have to take holiday. But children pick up a lot of bugs and you are likely to find that she gets everything going for a while after she starts. Work out a few back-up plans in case you need them. Most nurseries will insist your baby stays at home for 24-48 hours after their last episode of vomiting or diarrhea.

★ If you want to keep breastfeeding, you will need to stock up on expressed milk. Start getting your baby used to drinking from a bottle or a cup, as it may take a while for her to get used to it. You may prefer to offer your baby formula milk while you are away and breastfeed in the mornings and evenings. It will take a few days for your milk supply to adjust.

★ Always prepare your baby's bag the night before. This gives you extra time in the morning, which you will be grateful for! Remember to pack a favourite toy or blanket that he can keep with him to remind him of home while he is away.

★ If your baby cries when you leave her it can be heartbreaking. Try to give her a big kiss and go, rather than waiting to comfort her. Ask her carer to phone you when she has settled down – usually it is only a few minutes after you have gone.

Flexible working

If you do not want to go back to work full time there are a range of options that you could discuss with your employers.

★ Part time – working fewer hours per day or fewer days per week.
★ Working from home – either all the time, or just every now and then.
★ Compressed hours – working your hours but in fewer, longer days.
★ Flexi-time – having more flexible hours around a core work day.
★ Staggered hours – your start, break and leave times will be different.
★ Job share – when you share your job with another part-time worker.
★ Annualised hours – your hours are worked out over a year, with certain set shifts and other more flexible hours.

18 to 24 Months+

Your baby's development

Your child has been spending time developing his physical skills so that he can run, walk and climb. Now his memory is improving, his vocabulary growing and his social side is starting to bloom. You may find yourself getting frustrated by your child's new bids for independence, but it's all a natural part of growing up and finding his way in the world.

Your child's growth will come in fits and starts during this stage of his development, although he will probably grow more during spring and summer and slow down during the colder months.

Eighteen months

Your baby will be rushing around all over the place and may be getting more reluctant to go down for a nap in the daytime. He wants to be the centre of attention and will try to join in with your telephone calls or chats with friends.

Nineteen months

Your baby may enjoy learning to kick a ball, or trying to throw it into a bucket. He will be fascinated by stacking objects, jigsaw puzzles and ride-along toys. He should be able to communicate with short sentences such as 'Me do!' or 'More milk!'

Twenty months

At this age your baby will be very affectionate, and love helping you out around the house. However, he may also start to show a tendency towards more aggressive behaviour such as biting and pushing other children. It's your job to gently teach him right from wrong.

Twenty-one months

Your child may start to show a preference for 'boy' toys or 'girl' toys around this age, although for many children it's not until the age of three years that they start to notice gender differences. Celebrate your child's interests, rather than discouraging your boy from playing with dolls or your girl with trucks.

Twenty-two months

At this age, your child may start developing his own rituals, and become annoyed when things are done differently. Try to remain patient as you encourage him to try new things – toddlers can be very resistant to change.

Twenty-three months

Your baby will be able to hum and sing and his drawings and his scribbles will start to have more shape. His speech is developing quickly and he should be able to say three-word sentences, such as 'Where dog gone?'

Twenty-four months

Happy birthday to your two year old! You can now have a conversation, enjoy watching him run around the park and share lots of smiles and laughs. Take time to dig out some baby photo albums and look through them with him. You will be amazed to see how his personality and sense of independence has grown.

Your child will start to enjoy arranging things in categories and may learn to jump

Your child will be able to take off her own clothes

Your child will be able to use a spoon and fork

Your child will learn to kick and throw a ball and know a range of single words and talk in short sentences

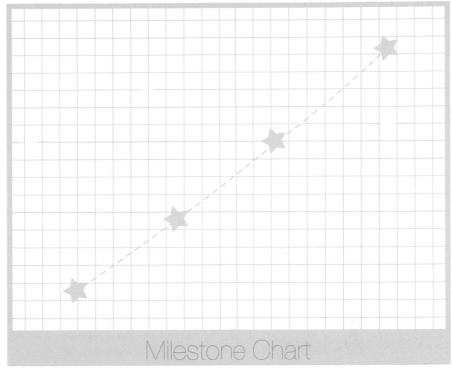

Milestone Chart

| 18-24 months | 19 months | 20 months | 24 months |

Some toddlers seem to develop a permanent cold during the winter months. This is because their immune system has not had a chance to develop any immunity to all the different types of virus flying around at this time of year.

Try to keep your language as positive as possible when talking to your child. For example 'Sit on the chair' is better than 'Don't stand on the chair' – and is more likely to get a positive result.

Fussy eaters

After your toddler reaches the age of one, her weight gain will slow down and this will affect her appetite. She may eat lots at some meals, and nothing at others, but this is normal. Most young children go through phases of fussy eating, for a variety of reasons. Some may be trying to show their independence and assert their authority, others may be experiencing neophobia – a fear of new things.

If you get anxious, you may find that mealtimes become stressful which will not help the situation. Don't worry too much about what your child eats in a single meal, think about what she eats over the course of a week. If you are concerned, you could buy vitamin supplements that are designed for young children and try some of these hints and tips.

Three fun ideas for snack time

1 **Fruit rainbow** – arrange fruit in a rainbow shape, using all the colours: Red – strawberries, orange – oranges, yellow – bananas, green – melon, blue – blueberries, purple – grapes .

2 **Ants on a log** – fill celery sticks with cream cheese and top with raisins.

3 **Rice cake faces** – spread peanut butter on a rice cake then add a face using grapes, cheese or chopped apple.

Don't bribe your child with the offer of pudding – this will make her want the savoury course even less.

Involve your child in mealtimes. You could ask her to pick what she would like to eat from a choice of two or three things, take her shopping for food, or ask her to help you with the cooking.

Offer one new food at a time so that your child doesn't feel overwhelmed. Don't make a fuss if she doesn't eat it, wait a few days and try again.

Eat as a family. Children learn how to eat by copying their parents and other children. As you eat, say positive things about the food, like 'This is delicious!'

Turn off the television. Your child will be distracted and unable to concentrate on eating.

Stick to a routine of meal and snack times. Young children like knowing what to expect.

Keep your child's portions small. She may be overwhelmed if there is a lot on her plate and you can always offer more if she eats everything there.

Praise your child when she eats well, and try not to give her attention when she is not eating. Toddlers like attention – even if it is negative. If she doesn't eat well, take the uneaten food away without commenting.

Some children have no room for food at mealtimes because they have had too much milk or sweetened drinks during the day. Try only offering water between meals.

Arrange for your child to eat with other children. She might eat better when she is with her own age group.

Keep mealtimes to a set length. Most toddlers eat what they are going to eat in the first 20 minutes of a meal and there's not much point carrying on any longer. Encourage them to eat for this amount of time, then take away the food that is left and offer them a piece of fruit or a yoghurt to end the meal.

Late bedtimes and early starts

By the time your child is older, he may well be sleeping for a large chunk of the night without waking. But you may find that it is harder to get him to go to bed in the evening than it was before… It could be that he is asserting his independence, or that he just finds the world so interesting that he can't bear to go to sleep in case he misses something. You can tell that he is tired by the way he yawns, rubs his eyes and gets frustrated and angry at the slightest thing. Or, it could be the way he is running around the house and bouncing on the sofa with the kind of energy that only comes from extreme exhaustion! Remember that you are the adult and you are in charge – even if it doesn't feel like it sometimes! Try some of these tips for a smoother bedtime.

Nightmares

Your child may start to have nightmares at this age, so be careful what television programmes he sees or books he reads before bed. Comfort your child if he wakes up and don't get cross or tell him he is being silly. Stay with him until he is calm, let him talk about the dream if he wants to, then gently encourage him to go back to sleep.

Keeping your child up later will not make him sleepier at bedtime. A lot of children find it harder to go to sleep if they are overtired and will actually go down easier when put to bed earlier. Aim for somewhere between 7 and 8 o'clock.

Don't be tempted to drop your child's nap. Instead, try to keep the nap as regular as possible and, if your child refuses to sleep, insist that he has 'quiet time' in his room instead.

A bedtime routine is important, but shouldn't be longer than 15 minutes. Any longer and your child may get a second wind. Stick to calming activities – bath, short story, bed – keeping it simple and most importantly, consistent every night.

Teach your child to fall asleep alone. If he will only go to sleep while you sit next to the bed this is a hard habit to break. Let him know that you are close by and will come if he needs you, but aim to leave the room so he can drop off alone.

Early starts

Work out what your child will call you back into the room to ask for, such as a favourite toy, a drink of water, or the potty. Make sure that you have incorporated them all into your bedtime routine before you put him in bed.

If your child is waking up very early in the morning, you could consider buying a sleep-training clock. This can be set so that a picture on the front changes from a night to a day scene at whatever time you choose. Try telling your child that he must not get out of bed until this happens. If your child's room is very light in the morning, drape a blanket over the curtains to keep out the light.

If your child is still in his cot, you might want to move him into a bed. Make a big fuss as you tell him how he is grown up enough to stay in his own bed at nighttime. Praise him for staying in bed but don't get angry if he keeps getting out. Just lead him back to bed firmly but gently. You may have to do this a few times until he gets the message.

If your child is testing his independence, try offering him simple choices, such as what pyjamas he wants to wear or story he wants to hear. If you usually read two short stories before bed, try reading one short story, then asking if he wants to go to sleep now or hear another story. If he chooses the second option – that's fine!

Try to stand your ground calmly and firmly. Don't get angry or give in to any tantrums. Children want attention – even if it is negative. If you are very frustrated, go into another room for a short while until you are calmer, so that your child doesn't see.

Your baby's speech

By the age of 18 months, your child will be able to say around 12 easily understandable words, such as 'milk', 'mama' and 'dada'. She will now start to link two words together to make simple sentences, such as 'want milk' or 'all gone'. Her vocabulary is not large, but she will be able to make herself understood using gestures and her tone of voice when she speaks. For example, when she says: 'Toy?' making a palms-up shrug, she is asking where her toy is. When she says: 'Toy!' in a demanding tone, pointing to the toy, she is asking for it to be handed over.

Make sure that you heap praise on everything that your child says, and echo the words back to her to reinforce them. Try not to correct her mistakes, as this will not help her confidence – she needs to feel that she can try out new words. Instead, you should model the right version of the word back to her when you reply. For example, if she says: "Want bittit!" you should hand her the biscuit and say: 'Okay, here is a biscuit." It's likely that your child will actively encourage you to tell her the names of the things around her, pointing to pictures in books, her toys or things that you see when you are out and about.

By the age of 24 months, your child will be able to understand between 200 and 500 words and say over 50, constructing sentences with two or three words. For example: 'More juice please'. She will be able to pronounce most vowels and the consonant sounds b,p,t,d,n,m,h,and w. Other words with consonants that she hasn't quite mastered are likely to be changed to fit in with her abilities. For example, 'grandma' becomes 'dama' and 'bubble' becomes 'bubba'. Children will also often miss the ends off words at this stage and usually can be understood about half of the time, especially by people used to listening and responding to them.

Talking troubles?

The age at which children learn to talk can vary, so don't worry if your child is not talking as much as you hoped. As long as your child is communicating in other ways, such as pointing at things, and following simple instructions that you give her, then she is on the right path. She may say 'no' a lot, but this is a normal part of asserting her independence. If your child has been learning more than one language at home, she may get confused and mix the two together, or use one for speaking more than the other, even though she seems to understand the spoken words of each language equally. This won't affect her ability to talk and may even improve her later academic ability.

If you are concerned about your child's language development or speech, you should talk to your health visitor or doctor. They will have a series of checks that will test your child's abilities and can recommend a hearing test if they feel it is necessary. In some cases, a delay in learning to talk can be a sign of autism.

Increasing understanding

Between 18 and 24 months, your child will be able to think and talk about things that he can't see. For example, she will know that her boots are by the door, or her yoghurt is in the fridge and will be able to go into a different room to find them. Try playing hide-and-seek games to test this new skill, your child will love searching for a toy that you have hidden in the room.

Learning through play

Play is one of the most important ways your child develops – it's how he learns to interact with the world. Experts recommend that toddlers' play should be creative, social and active. Your child should get at least an hour of physical activity a day to help his muscles, bones, heart and lungs develop. If it's a rainy day, try dancing in the house, go to a soft-play area, or consider buying a baby trampoline!

Eighteen months

Your child will love toys that help him play make-believe games, such as a doctor's bag or tool kit, a baby doll with a bath or buggy, or plastic cups, saucers, spoons and picnic rug. You can buy plastic or wooden food to play shops, or draw your favourite food items on strong card and use these instead.

Nineteen months

Make a dressing-up box and fill it with old hats, scarves, jewellery and bags. If you don't have many, visit charity shops or jumble sales and see what you can find. Spend time dressing up and acting out different parts with your child, using funny voices as you role-play.

Twenty months

Crayons are good for young children, as they are easier to hold than pens – and arguably less messy. Let your child make lots of dots, dashes and circles on pieces of paper with bright colours then, when he has finished, help him to paint a wash of watery black paint over the top. This will make his patterns really stand out!

Twenty-one months

Your child will love to play with balls – a foam ball or beach ball is lighter to carry around and less likely to hurt anyone who gets hit. Try simple back and forwards kicking between each other, kicking at a wall and counting or just let her try to dribble the ball as you pretend to chase her around the park – toddlers adore playing chase!

Twenty-two months

A standing up and sitting down game, like 'Ring Around the Roses' or 'Musical Bumps', is bound to make your child laugh. Play some music or sing to your child and let her know that when you stop, she has to sit down on a cushion as quickly as possible.

Twenty-three months

Look through a pile of magazines together, and carefully cut out the pictures that your child is interested in. (Keep the scissors away from him!) Spend time together making a collage with them, using non-toxic glue and the cardboard from a cereal packet as a backing board.

Twenty-four months

Put on some music and dance together, pretending to be different animals. You can flutter your arms like a butterfly, scurry around like a mouse, stamp like an elephant or roar like a lion – but make sure you get your child to join in and copy you. You could end the game with a pretend chase and tickle as you pretend to be a crocodile who is going to snap your baby up!

Playing with others

You may notice that your toddler favours one type of play over another. Some children are more drawn to quiet play, while others prefer rushing about! Your child is not old enough to play with other children yet, but it is a good idea to arrange playdates so she gets used to being around other children and can engage in parallel play. This is when your child sits and plays beside another similar-aged child without interacting. They seem to be ignoring one other and remain engrossed in their own activities, but this is a natural part of learning to play together.

When you arrange a playdate, be aware that your toddler might:

- Act like she owns certain objects.
- Want to do things without help.
- Have trouble sharing.
- Say "no" and "mine" a lot.
- Hit, push, bite or grab to keep toys.
- Be wary of adults she doesn't know.
- Have mood swings and tantrums.
- Dislike changes in his routines.

But she will also be able to:

- Show concern for others.
- Share food and toys if encouraged.
- Use a security toy or blanket to self-comfort if she gets upset.

Your child is starting to understand that her actions have consequences. A playdate is a good opportunity to start teaching her good behaviour. Try to praise good behaviour where possible, and ignore minor upsets and accidents. If your child hurts another child, tell her that she must not hurt others and explain why as simply as you can. For example, 'Theo is sad because you hit him.'

Ways to help your child

★ Talk to your child about new things you are going to do before they happen to help her prepare herself.

★ Arrange playdates at your house and at other children's houses.

★ Let her help you with chores around the house and give her lots of praise.

★ Choose stories to read together that talk about emotions, feelings and consequences.

★ Encourage your child to talk about her emotions, and give her the words to explain how she feels. For example, 'I think you are feeling sad because you are crying.' Then offer a way of helping her. For example, 'Would you like a hug to help you feel better?' If she resists the hug, don't force it. Say 'I can see you would like to be left alone for a while.' She will come for the hug in her own time.

Stages of play

★ Solitary play is when your toddler plays by herself.

★ Parallel play is when your toddler plays beside another child without interacting.

★ Imitative play is when your toddler and another child copy each other. For example, one starts to jump and the other joins in.

★ Social bids. Your toddler will offer toys to other children as a way of communicating.

★ Co-operative play. Your toddler plays with other children. Many children are not ready for this until 36 months.

Out and about

It's good to get out with your baby, and now that he is walking, you don't have to take the buggy. Days out don't have to be expensive for you both to have fun – your child will find all sorts of simple activities stimulating and inspiring. Try some of these ideas if you're stuck for a morning's entertainment or you just want a break from the local playground.

Take a baby-led walk

Leave the house and let your child take the lead. See where he wants to go and what he wants to do – he will love the feeling of being in control. If he wants to pick up leaves, play with gravel, look in shop windows, or stop to examine your neighbour's walls, then that's fine. You will get a chance to see the world from his perspective.

Go shopping

Take your child to a local charity shop and let him browse. Tell him that you can buy him one thing – it shouldn't cost very much. Steer him towards the children's clothes and toys section, but don't be surprised if you end up with something like a wooden letter rack – it's his choice!

Make a collection

Go for a walk around your local area and make a collection of things that you find. For example, leaves and stones from the park or shells or stones if you live near the beach. At the end of the walk you can take them home, clean them and arrange them together in a cardboard box or on a shelf.

Camping in the garden

Put up a tent, get your sleeping bags out and pretend you are going camping. Take your lunch outside and eat it in the tent. Take your child's teddies and dollies too, with lots of blankets so that you can tuck them up in the tent and read them a story.

Use your local library

A trip to the library is always fun – and free! Spend time looking through books together

and then choose your favourite ones to take home. Many libraries have tables where you can sit and do some colouring together too.

Museums and galleries

Your child will love exploring a local museum even at this young age. Try to follow him lead, stopping when he does and talking to him about the things that he seems interested in, rather than trying to make him look at the things you think he should be looking at.

Soft play area

Visit your local soft play area and enjoy watching your child climb, jump and whizz down slides. Some soft play areas are open all week, others just on certain days, so check online or in the local newspaper.

Take the train

Take your child on a train ride – you don't have to go more than a couple of stops before getting off and coming home again. Explain what you are doing, let your child hold his own ticket and choose his seat. It's not a trip to nowhere – it's a voyage of discovery!

Farms and fruit

A visit to a child-friendly farm always makes a great day out. Some farms offer seasonal fruit-picking which is always a favourite with small children, although it's worth keeping an eye on the amount of fruit that ends up in their stomachs!

Pick a pet shop

Just because you visit a pet shop, it doesn't mean that you have to buy anything! Your child will love looking at the fish and rabbits, and you may find one that has a viewing window to watch the larger animals being groomed.

Dealing with tantrums

Every child throws a tantrum at some point; it's a natural part of growing up. Most children have fewer tantrums as they grow older and find it easier to use language to communicate what they want and have more of an understanding about how the world works. The way that you deal with tantrums is important. If you shout and smack your child, or ignore the emotions that she is struggling to deal with, you could make them worse. Well-known tricks for helping you deal with tantrums like star charts, time out and naughty steps work well for older children, but are unlikely to have too much effect on younger toddlers.

Tips for managing a tantrum

Ignore

Toddlers love to be the centre of attention, and they don't really mind if the attention they are getting is positive or negative. If you make a big fuss when your child behaves badly, this may actually make it worth their while. So, if the tantrum is small, and your child is somewhere safe where she won't hurt herself, simply leave the room and wait for the tantrum to subside.

Distract

Distracting your child is only likely to work in the early stages of a tantrum, but can be a surprisingly good way of stopping a full-blown attack. If you are outside, point out something you can see. Try 'Wow, is that a green lorry?' or 'Can you see that spider?' If you are inside, you could grab one of your child's favourite toys and make it talk to her, using a funny voice.

Leave

If you are out at the shops, in a café or the playground, put down whatever you were going to buy and leave. Take your child to a quiet spot and wait for her to calm down. Once she is calm, you can talk about what triggered the tantrum, in simple language, but don't force it if she doesn't want to talk.

Be consistent

Never make a threat that you can't follow through. If you say 'I'm going to leave you here forever,' or 'We won't go on holiday' it won't work in the long run, because you have no intention of carrying it out. Instead, stick to a logical consequence for your child's actions – something that is relevant to the situation you are in. For example, you could take

Tantrum do's and don'ts

* DO toddler-proof your house by putting dangerous or breakable things out of reach.

* DON'T ever give in. If you have said no, stick with the no. If a tantrum results in you changing your mind and saying yes, your child has learned that this is a good way to get results and will try it again.

* DO look out for ways to give lots of praise and attention all the times your child does something good.

* DON'T wait till things get out of hand. If you can see a tantrum brewing it's better to step in and defuse the situation sooner rather than later.

* DO have clear routines so that your child knows what to expect and what is coming next.

* DON'T keep saying no. Try 'later' or 'another day' or 'after your nap.'

* DO make sure that your child is getting enough time to let off steam during the day. For example, dancing to music at home or running around the park.

* DON'T shout back. Too much yelling from you sets a bad example and makes tantrums worse.

* DO use humour if you can. A tickle or a silly face at the right time can stop a tantrum in its tracks.

* DON'T let your child think she has no control. Offer her simple choices about the food she eats or clothes she wears.

* DO pay attention your child's feelings. A lot of her frustration will come from the sense that she is not being understood. Try 'I know that you feel sad' or 'I can see you're angry about that.'

* DON'T spring surprises on her. If you have to leave the playground or a friend's house give her a several warnings – for example ten minute, five minutes, one minute.

a favourite toy away for a short while, or make her sit in the hallway until she has calmed down.

Be prepared

If you know you are entering a 'danger area' where your child often has tantrums, work out a plan before you go in. For example, if she always has a meltdown in the supermarket, tell her beforehand that she can choose a magazine at the end of the trip, if she is good while you shop.

Planning another baby

Only you and your partner can decide it's the right time for another baby. There's no right or wrong age gap – everyone will have an opinion, but what works for some families won't work for others. It may be a harder decision to make than whether to have a first child, because you have more of an idea what's involved, and because you will be changing the dynamics of your new family. A new baby will affect your finance, work, relationships and your other children, and many mothers say that a second child is actually more than double the work. Having a second baby too soon after your first can be hard on your body, and studies show that it's a good idea to wait 18 to 23 months after the birth before conceiving. Having gaps smaller than 18 months and over 59 months are both associated with an increased risk of having a baby prematurely and with a lower birth weight.

Short age gap
(18 months or below)

Cons
- Looking after your first child while you are pregnant is tiring.
- After the new baby arrives, you'll be feeding, cleaning and changing two babies.
- You'll need to get a second cot and a double buggy.

Pros
- Your first child won't be old enough to be very jealous.
- You'll get the feeding, cleaning and changing over and done with in one go (unless you have more!)
- Your children should play well together when they are older and will be doing similar things at the same time.
- If you're 38 years old and you want more children, you might not be able to wait too long. Many women can still get pregnant in their early 40s but fertility rates drop dramatically after 35.

Medium age gap
(2 to 3 years)

Cons
- Your first child is likely to be jealous and there may be later rivalry
- Your first child may start toilet training just as you start changing your new baby's nappies
- There may be a conflict between what each child needs – for example, your firstborn wants to run round the park but you have to feed your baby.

Pros
- Your body has had time to recover from the first pregnancy.
- You have more time to enjoy each of your children's baby days.
- You won't need to buy a new buggy or cot.

Long age gap
(5 years and over)

Cons
⭐ The broken nights, continual feeding and nappy changing may come as a shock.

⭐ It may be hard trying to juggle both your children's needs, as they are unlikely to want to play with the same toys or watch the same programmes on TV.

Pros
⭐ Your older child can help out with the new baby.

⭐ You'll be able to enjoy each child more as an individual.

You're pregnant!

⭐ It's up to you to decide when to tell your child they are expecting a new baby brother or sister, but it's a good idea not to leave it until the last minute. Your child is more likely to cope better if he is prepared. Spend time reading books about new babies together, and have a look through photo albums of your child as a baby. If you have friends with small babies you could pay them a visit.

⭐ Second labours are often quicker than the first, so plan childcare for you firstborn in advance. If he has never spent much time away from you, you may want to let him practise having overnight stays with the friends or relatives who are going to help you out.

⭐ If the birth of your first baby was traumatic, you might want to ask your midwife about how you could do things differently. She may suggest talking to a trained counsellor who can go through the notes from your first birth with you, and help you move on from the experience.

Common health problems and first aid tips

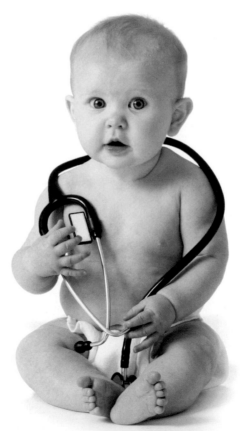

First aid for babies and young children

How to stop a baby from choking

If your baby is choking but coughing, let him cough as this is the best way to clear his airway. Do not pat his back or offer water. However, if something is lodged in his throat that is stopping him breathing, take immediate action.

If your baby is conscious:

1 Give five back blows.

Baby: Sit or kneel and support the child on your lap. Support him in a head-downwards position. Don't compress the soft tissues under the jaw as this will make the obstruction worse. Give up to five sharp back blows with the heel of one hand in the middle of the back between the shoulder blades.

Child over 1: Back blows are more effective if the child is positioned head down. Put a small child across your lap as you would a baby. If this isn't possible, support your child in a forward-leaning position and give the back blows from behind.

2 If your baby is still choking, give five thrusts. Each thrust is a separate attempt to dislodge the object.

Baby: Support him on your arm, which is placed down (or across) your thigh as you sit or kneel. Find his breastbone, and place two fingers in the middle. Give five sharp chest thrusts (pushes), compressing the chest by about a third.

Child over 1: Stand or kneel behind your child. Place your arms under his arms and around his upper abdomen. Clench your fist and place it between his navel and ribs. Grasp this hand with your other hand and pull sharply inwards and upwards. Repeat up to five times. Don't apply pressure to the lower ribcage as this may cause damage.

3 If the object is not cleared, call an ambulance and continue back blows and chest thrusts until help arrives.

If your baby is unconscious:

Open the airway, give five breaths and start CPR (see next page).

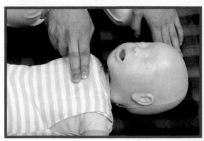

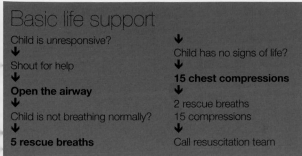

Basic life support

Child is unresponsive? ↓
↓
Shout for help ↓
↓
Open the airway
↓
Child is not breathing normally?
↓
5 rescue breaths

Child has no signs of life?
↓
15 chest compressions
↓
2 rescue breaths
15 compressions
↓
Call resuscitation team

How to give CPR*

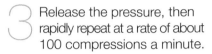

It is a good idea to make time to attend a course in baby first aid where you will learn how to follow this procedure correctly. Ask your midwife or health visitor for details.

Open the airway

Baby: Ensure his head is in a neutral position, with head and neck in line and not tilted. At the same time, with your fingertips under the point of his chin, lift the chin.

Child over 1: Leave him in the position you found him. Place your hand on his forehead and gently tilt the head back. At the same time, with your fingertips under the point of his chin, lift the chin. This may be easier if he is on his back.

Note: Don't push on the soft tissues under the chin as this may block the airway. If you think there may have been an injury to the neck, tilt the head carefully, a small amount at a time, until the airway is open.

Rescue breaths

Baby: Ensure his head is in a neutral position and lift the chin. Take a breath and cover his mouth and nose with your mouth, making sure it's sealed. Blow five breaths steadily into his mouth and nose over 1 – 1.5 seconds. It should be sufficient to make the chest visibly rise. Keeping his head tilted and chin lifted, take your mouth away and watch for his chest to fall as

air comes out. Take another breath and repeat sequence five times.

Child over 1: Tilt his head and lift the chin. Close the soft part of his nose using the index finger and thumb of the hand that's on his forehead. Open his mouth a little but keep the chin pointing upwards. Take a breath and place your lips around his mouth, making sure it's sealed. Blow five breaths steadily into his mouth over 1 – 1.5 seconds, watching for the chest to rise. Keeping his head tilted and chin lifted, take your mouth away and watch for the chest to fall as air comes out. Take another breath and repeat sequence five times. Check that his chest rises and falls as if he was breathing normally.

Chest compressions

Compress the breastbone.

1. To avoid compressing the stomach, find the point where the lowest ribs join in the middle, and then one finger's width above that.

2. Push down by roughly one-third of the depth of the chest.

3. Release the pressure, then rapidly repeat at a rate of about 100 compressions a minute.

4. For babies, give 1 breath to 3 compressions, and for children give 2 breaths to 15 compressions. After the compressions, tilt the head and give the effective breaths.

5. Continue at a ratio of 1 breath to 3 compressions for babies and 2 breaths to 15 compressions for children.

6. Continue resuscitation until your child shows signs of life or qualified help arrives.

Baby: Do the compressions on the breastbone with the tips of two fingers, not the whole hand or with two hands.

Child over 1: Place the heel of one hand over the lower third of the breastbone. Lift the fingers to ensure that pressure is not applied over the ribs. Position yourself vertically above the chest and, with your arm straight, compress the breastbone so that you push it down by approx. one-third of the depth of the chest. In larger children, or if you're small, this may be done more easily by using both hands with the fingers interlocked, avoiding pressure on the ribs.

* Cardiopulmonary resusciation

Accidents and emergencies

Bleeding

⭐ Press firmly on the wound with a clean cloth, such as a flannel, for about 10 minutes or until the bleeding stops.

⭐ Raising an injured limb will help stop bleeding. Do not do this if you think the limb may be broken.

⭐ Cover the wound with a clean dressing.

⭐ If the bleeding won't stop or the wound is gaping, take your child to A&E.

Convulsions

If your child turns blue and becomes rigid with staring or rolling eyes, or twitching limbs, he is having a fit. Stay calm. Most fits will stop within three minutes, and will not cause brain damage. Fits are common in children under the age of three.

⭐ Lie your child on their side to make sure he doesn't vomit or choke.

⭐ When the fit is over, reassure your child, make him comfortable and call a doctor.

⭐ If the fit hasn't stopped within three minutes, call an ambulance.

Burns and scalds

⭐ Put the burn or scald under running cold water to reduce the heat in the skin. Don't do this for longer than 10 minutes.

⭐ Don't use butter, toothpaste, oil or ointment which will have to be cleaned off before the skin can be treated.

⭐ Use something clean to cover the burn or scald. For example, cling film or a clean tea towel.

⭐ If your child's clothes are stuck to the skin, don't try to take them off.

⭐ If the burn is very bad, take your child to A&E.

Electrocution

Turn off the power before approaching your child. If you can't do this, don't touch him, but use a wooden or plastic object to push him away from the source of the shock. If your child is unresponsive, start the CPR sequence. (See previous page.)

Swallowing poisons or medicine

⭐ Stay calm and keep your child calm.

⭐ Take your child to A&E, with the tablets, or bottle so that the doctors know what he has swallowed.

⭐ Keep watching your child and remind yourself of how to resuscitate him using CPR if he becomes unconscious. (See previous page.)

⭐ Don't do anything to try and make your child throw up.

⭐ If your child's mouth is sore or blistered, make him sip milk on the way to the hospital.

Broken bones

⭐ Do not try to move your child.
⭐ Call an ambulance.

Call an ambulance if your child:

- stops breathing.
- is struggling for breath.
- is unconscious or seems unaware of what's going on.
- won't wake up.
- has a fit for the first time, even if they seem to recover.

Take your child to A&E if they:

- have a fever and are lethargic despite having children's paracetamol or ibuprofen.
- are having difficulty breathing.
- have severe abdominal pain.
- have a cut that won't stop bleeding.
- have a leg or arm injury and can't use the limb.
- have swallowed a poison or tablets.
- have an object lodged in their nose or ear. Leave the object where it is or you risk pushing it further in.

When your baby is unwell

Diarrhoea

Your baby may have diarrhoea if his stools are loose and watery, a greenish colour or foul-smelling. It could be caused by an infection, a food allergy or poisoning. Give your baby milk or cooled, boiled water to prevent dehydration, as this may require hospital treatment.

Signs of dehydration include:

- Fewer wet nappies
- Dry mouth
- Irritability
- Drowsiness
- Sunken soft spot on the top of his head
- Skin that doesn't spring back when gently pinched

If your child is on solid foods, switch to bland, starchy foods like bananas, stewed apple and rice cereal until the diarrhoea stops. If you are breastfeeding, try to cut out foods that may be a trigger. This includes:

- Greasy foods
- High fibre foods
- Dairy products
- Food with a high sugar content

If your baby's diarrhoea is caused by a viral or bacterial infection it will be contagious. Wash your hands thoroughly with soap and water after caring for your baby, and keep all surfaces around the changing table disinfected.

Vomiting

Many babies bring up small amounts of milk while or after they are being fed. This is called posseting and is not a cause for alarm.

If your child is vomiting, you should watch him carefully. Check for signs of dehydration (see above) and make sure he keeps drinking fluids. The most common cause is likely to be gastroenteritis, which also causes diarrhoea. Your child will be able to fight off the infection after a few days.

Call a doctor if your child:

- has been vomiting for more than 24 hours
- has not been able to hold down fluids for the last eight hours
- is floppy, irritable, off their food or not their usual self
- has severe stomach pain
- has a headache and stiff neck

Constipation

Your baby may be constipated if he is producing hard, dry stools less often than normal. Offer him plenty of extra fluids, but check with your doctor before using anything to ease his discomfort.

Fever

If your child's face feels hot to the touch, or they look red and flushed, they may have a fever. Measured under the arm, normal temperature is about 36.4°C (97.4°F). A fever is a temperature of over 37.5°C.

Taking your baby's temperature:

- Some digital thermometers are designed to use in the rectum, in the mouth or in the ear. With a young baby it is easiest and safest to take his temperature under his arm.
- First wipe under the arm to remove any sweat then place the bulb of the thermometer in the fold of his armpit.
- Hold his arm against his side to keep the thermometer in place. Leave it for three or four minutes, or until it beeps to tell you it is ready.

Note: Do not use a strip thermometer, as this measures the temperature of your baby's skin only. If you have an old mercury-in-glass thermometer, dispose of it carefully and buy a digital thermometer instead.

Contact your doctor if your baby's temperature is 38°C (101°F) or higher if they're under three months, or your baby's temperature is 39°C (102°F) or higher if they're three to six months.

Note: Don't take your baby's temperature after his bath – wait 20 minutes for an accurate reading.

To treat a fever:

- Keep your baby hydrated, even if he doesn't seem to want to drink.
- Don't give him food unless he wants it.
- Undress him to his nappy.
- Open a window or adjust the heating.
- Give your baby baby paracetamol or ibuprofen.
- Always check the dosage instructions on the bottle.

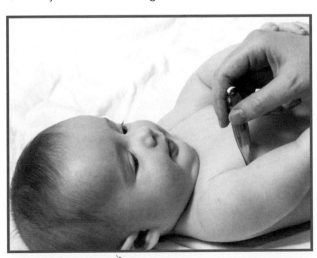

Common childhood illnesses

Conjunctivitis

Conjunctivitis is a common eye condition, also known as red eye or pink eye. Symptoms include itchiness, watering and inflammation and sometimes a sticky coating on the eyelashes. It should clear up in a few days, but some cases may require antibiotic eye-drops. If a newborn baby has conjuncitivits take him to see a doctor immediately.

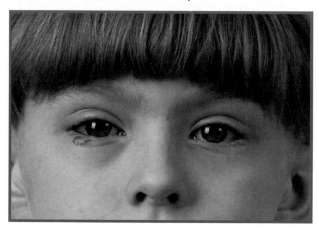

Croup

Croup is a virus, which causes your child to cough with a barking sound like a seal and usually lasts for around one week. Severe cases may need treating in hospital.

Meningitis

Meningitis is an inflammation of the meninges, membranes that cover the brain and spinal cord. Viral meningitis is more common and less serious, with symptoms similar to flu. Bacterial meningitis is rare but can be life-threatening. If you suspect your child has meningitis, you should seek help immediately.

Symptoms of meningitis:

- fever
- lethargy
- irritability
- headache
- sensitivity to light
- stiff neck
- rash
- fits

A newborn may also have:

- jaundice
- stiffness of body and neck
- fever with cold feet and hands
- high pitched cry
- bulging soft spots on top of his head
- irritation at being touched

Note: If your child has a rash, do the glass test: Press the side of a clear glass firmly against the skin. A fever with a rash that does not fade under pressure is a sign of meningococcal septicaemia and is an emergency. Acting fast could save your child's life.

Using a glass to check for meningitis

Mumps

Mumps is a contagious viral infection that used to be common in children. Painful swellings appear under the ears at the side of the face and are accompanied by headache, fever and joint pain. If you suspect your child has mumps, you should call your doctor.

Note: All children should be vaccinated against mumps.

Oral thrush

Oral thrush is most common in babies under 6 months. You may notice cracked skin in the corners of your baby's mouth or white patches on the lips, tongue or inside of the cheeks. Some babies may find it hard to feed, as their mouths are sore. If you are bottle-feeding or using a dummy, clean them in hot, soapy water after each use. If you are breastfeeding and your nipples are red and sore, you may have thrush in your nipples and be passing it to your baby. Your doctor can prescribe an anti-fungal treatment for you and your baby.

Tonsillitis

Tonsillitis is an inflammation of the tonsils, which become enlarged and red with a yellow or white coating. Your child will have a sore throat, fever, swollen neck glands and have difficulty swallowing. He will find it hard to eat, so should be given soup, milkshakes, ice cream and smoothies instead of solid food. Your doctor can tell you if the tonsillitis is caused by a virus or strep bacteria. If it is the latter, they will prescribe antibiotics.

Whooping Cough

Whooping cough is a bacterial infection that can cause your child to cough so hard and fast that he runs out of breath and has to inhale deeply, making a "whooping" noise. Around 50% of babies under the age of 12 months will need to go hospital. Adults who have whooping cough may not have severe symptoms, but can pass the infection on to children.

Note: All children should be vaccinated against whooping cough.

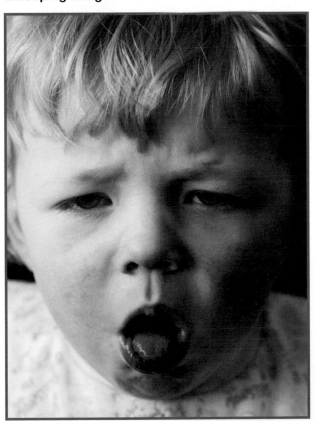

Childhood rashes

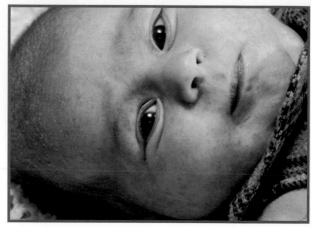

Eczema

Chickenpox

Chickenpox is a common viral illness. It starts as a rash of red, itchy spots that turn into fluid-filled blisters. These then form scabs, which drop off. Some children have a few spots, others have them all over their body. Ask your pharmacist for something to soothe the itching.

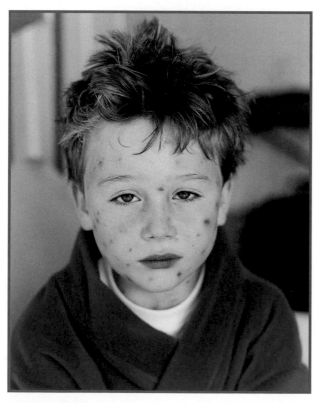

Chicken pox

Eczema

Eczema is a long-term condition that causes the skin to become itchy, red, dry and cracked. It commonly occurs behind the knees or on the front of the elbows. Try not to scratch as this will make it worse and ask your pharmacist to recommend soothing lotions and bath oils. If it becomes very bad, your doctor can prescribe steroid creams.

Hand, foot and mouth disease

Not to be confused with foot and mouth disease, this is a viral infection that is most common in young children. Symptoms include a fever and blisters or sores inside the mouth, on the palms and soles of the feet and on the buttocks. Hand, foot, and mouth disease may cause discomfort, but will pass on its own in a week to 10 days.

Impetigo

Impetigo is a bacterial skin infection, which is most common in children aged 2 to 6 years but can be caught by babies and adults too. It appears on the skin as clusters of itchy little bumps that weep fluid, forming a honey-colored crust. Touching the fluid can spread the infection. It is very contagious and your child will need antibiotics from the doctor to clear it up.

Measles

Measles is a contagious viral illness, which is most common in children aged between one and four years old. Your child will have a fever and cold symptoms as well as a red-brown spotty rash that usually starts behind his ears and spreads to the rest of the body.

Note: All children should be vaccinated against measles.

Scarlet fever

Scarlet fever is a rash that sometimes appears with a sore throat and high fever. The rash starts on the chest and abdomen and spreads all over the body.

It is bright red like sunburn and feels rough like sandpaper. Your child's tongue may have a whitish appearance, with bright red tastebuds. Scarlet fever was once a deadly childhood illness, but it is now easily cured with antibiotics from the doctor.

Slapped cheek syndrome

Also called fifth disease, this is a lacy red rash that appears on the face, torso or limbs. It is a viral infection and your child may complain of cold symptoms before it appears. Most children will not need treatment as this is usually a mild condition that passes in a few days. Occasionally it can last up to four or five weeks.

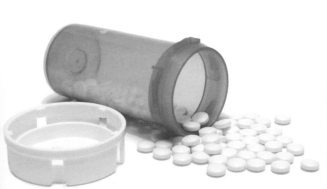

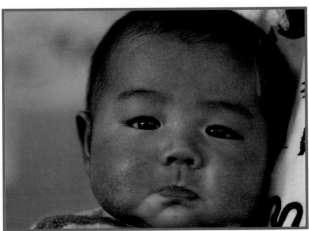

Slapped cheek syndrome

Index

Space for your notes

Doctor:

**Out of
hours
doctor:**

**Health
visitor:**

A&E: